Gambling on Humanitarian Intervention

Moral Hazard, Rebellion and Civil War

Edited by Timothy W. Crawford and
Alan J. Kuperman

 Routledge
Taylor & Francis Group

First published 2006 by Routledge
2 Park Square, Milton Park, Abingdon, Oxon, OX14 4RN

Simultaneously published in the USA and Canada by Routledge
270 Madison Ave, New York NY 10016

Routledge is an imprint of the Taylor & Francis Group

Transferred to Digital Printing 2008

© 2006 Taylor & Francis Ltd

Typeset in Times by Techset Composition Limited

British Library Cataloguing in Publication Data
A catalogue record for this book is available from the British Library

Library of Congress Cataloging in Publication Data
A catalog record for this book has been requested

ISBN10: 0-415-46374-2 (pbk)
ISBN10: 0-415-37946-6 (hbk)

ISBN13: 978-0-415-46374-4 (pbk)
ISBN13: 978-0-415-37946-5 (hbk)

Publisher's Note
The publisher has gone to great lengths to ensure the quality of this reprint but points out that some imperfections in the original may be apparent

Contents

Introduction: Debating the Hazards of Intervention

TIMOTHY W. CRAWFORD & ALAN J. KUPERMAN

The concept of moral hazard invites controversy because it appears to impugn the motives and character of seemingly innocent victims. It argues that, when people are protected by insurance, some of them will behave fraudulently or irresponsibly, becoming victims because of the resulting insurance payout. The controversy only intensifies when this logic is carried over to humanitarian military intervention, which can be seen as a type of insurance policy to protect sub-state groups from genocide and ethnic cleansing. The implication is that some groups engage in risky rebellions because they expect to benefit from international intervention if the state retaliates. In short, rebels provoke genocidal retaliation against their own group because of the expectation of humanitarian intervention.

This volume explores that controversial thesis by engaging several debates: the *definition* of moral hazard in the context of intervention; the theory's *theoretical* novelty and ability to describe and explain dynamics of internal conflict; its *empirical* record in recent cases of genocidal violence; and the *policy* implications for reforming the conduct of humanitarian intervention.

Debate starts with semantics because 'moral hazard' actually encompasses two different, though related, dynamics. The first occurs when over-insurance causes the insured to behave fraudulently—e.g. burning down one's house because the insurance pays more than the house's value. The second occurs when any insurance (not necessarily over-insurance) causes the insured to behave irresponsibly because it is not worth the effort to behave responsibly—e.g. parking one's car on the street rather than paying for a more secure garage because the car is fully ensured against vandalism. The original definition of 'moral hazard', which is still reflected in common usage, includes both dynamics. But some economists, and Robert Rauchhaus in his rational-choice contribution to this volume, insist that only the latter dynamic is moral hazard, whereas the former is a problem of inappropriate contracting. The distinction is interesting but, as another rationalist Harrison Wagner notes in his contribution, it is the former problem that is usually meant by the moral hazard of humanitarian intervention. He explains that vulnerable groups are unlikely to rebel if they expect intervention merely to cut the cost of failed rebellion. But they are more likely to rebel if they expect state retaliation to trigger a level of intervention on their behalf sufficient to enable achievement of otherwise unattainable political goals. As he puts it, "Calls for humanitarian military intervention are demands that outsiders participate in the renegotiation of the contracts that define a state".

Even if we accept this broader meaning of moral hazard, there remains a second definitional matter. Namely, if the prospect of intervention leads some groups to rebel and thereby provoke state retaliation, must that provocation be intentional? In other words, does the perception of over-insurance lead groups to behave fraudulently or only recklessly? As Alan Kuperman observes, most dictionary definitions of 'provoke' do not require intentionality, which matches his contention that the prospect of intervention can lead groups *either* intentionally to provoke or merely to run a high risk of provoking retaliation. (Interestingly, the distinctiveness of the latter definition evaporates as the risk approaches 100%.) This debate on intentionality is exemplified by the volume's opposing views of Bosnia's 1992 secession from Yugoslavia. Jon Western insists the republic's decision to declare independence was not intended to provoke the Serbs and thus did not arise from moral hazard. Kuperman, however, contends that Bosnia's Muslims consciously refrained from declaring the independence that would trigger war until receiving promises of international recognition, because they thought such recognition carried a guarantee of protection; thus moral hazard is indeed to blame. More generally, Timothy Crawford says that in order to blame moral hazard a rebellion must be both a perverse and unintended—though not necessarily unanticipated—consequence of intervention. Thus he implicates moral hazard whenever intervenors did not aim for or want rebellion, even if they anticipated it as a side-effect of their intervention. By contrast, Arman Grigorian and Rauchhaus argue that, if intervenors persist after realizing they are inciting rebellion, then moral hazard cannot be blamed.

Semantics aside, this volume raises important questions about the theoretical usefulness of moral hazard as a new explanation for the escalation of ethnic conflict. As Crawford explains, the notion of moral hazard is linked to three more general social science concepts that have already been applied in studies of conflict and intervention: perverse incentives, negative precedents and unintended consequences. Moreover, several of our authors discuss how moral hazard has been applied to international relations outside the realm of security, for example the bail-out of bankrupt states by the International Monetary Fund. But it is a recent innovation to apply moral hazard to questions of military intervention, rebellion and genocide—and this volume shows the new application to be fruitful in at least three ways. First, it reveals the inherently double-edged nature of humanitarian intervention. Second, as Crawford, Grigorian and Wagner illustrate, it can raise new and interesting questions concerning the causes of internal war and the consequences of intervention. Finally, as Kuperman and Rauchhaus demonstrate, the moral hazard analogy may generate prescriptions to mitigate the dark side of intervention.

Several authors, however, question whether the two-player model of moral hazard is the appropriate theoretical tool to understand what is in reality a three-player game involving sub-state groups, states and potential intervenors. Grigorian and Wagner note that, if states and sub-state groups both act rationally and share common expectations about the prospect of intervention, this prospect should have no net effect on the likelihood of violence between them but only on the ultimate bargain they reach, whether through war or peace. Western goes further by suggesting that a robust intervention regime could deter state violence, which would avert rebellions that he contends groups launch only in reaction to oppression. By contrast, Crawford and Kuperman argue that the prospect of intervention may embolden rebels without deterring states—because of factors such as domestic politics, biased perception, indivisibility of stakes and the rebels' tolerance of casualties and desire for power—thereby making violence more likely. Grigorian and Wagner concede that the prospect of future intervention may encourage states to perpetrate genocidal violence preventively, so as to eliminate domestic challengers before they can benefit from intervention, but they insist that this problem cannot be attributed to moral hazard. Yet the dynamic does stem directly from the increased proclivity of groups to rebel if they expect intervention, which is the problem of moral hazard. Accordingly, Crawford labels this a second-order effect, or 'thin' version, of moral hazard theory.

Empirically there is debate over how much recent inter-ethnic violence can be attributed to the moral hazard of humanitarian intervention, both in specific cases and across the universe of conflicts. Or, to phrase this as a question in social science parlance: even if moral hazard has been correctly identified as an independent variable, how much of the variance in violent outcomes does it explain? In his detailed case study of Kosovo, Grigorian acknowledges that the USA exacerbated violence but argues that this stemmed from a deliberate goal of punishing the Milosevic regime, rather than being a perverse consequence of a benign intervention policy designed to prevent violence, as Crawford and Kuperman contend.

Western offers another dissenting view, arguing that, both in the Balkans and more broadly, the causes of civil wars are so complex, involving long histories of jostling among groups seeking to maintain or usurp power, and struggles within those groups over how to do so, that the simple logic of moral hazard will explain very little, even if it appears to fit at a superficial level. He acknowledges that adversaries in internal conflict will almost always seek external intervention on their behalf, so that one can almost always find evidence suggestive of moral hazard, but he argues that it is not causally significant for the outbreak or perpetuation of violence. He also correctly observes that the prospect of humanitarian intervention cannot plausibly explain most historical cases of genocidal violence because they occurred well before such intervention even arguably became an emerging norm.

Crawford and Kuperman accept that moral hazard can explain only part of the story of violent internal conflict, but contend that it is an especially significant part because it is less than obvious and yet is very proximate to and decisive for the outcome of war. They concede that antecedent historical domestic processes of conflict escalation set the stage for potential violence. But they insist that such processes do not inevitably lead to internal war, which requires momentous decisions (agency) at key moments by states and sub-state groups. The least intuitive of these decisions, they say, is that of vulnerable groups to take up arms against stronger states that have threatened genocidal retaliation. (Indeed, the vast majority of the world's at-risk minority groups do not launch such rebellions.) Kuperman and Crawford say that governments should be expected to forcefully resist challenges to their authority, especially when rebels threaten the regime's monopoly on force. What they consider puzzling is why members of groups that are potentially so vulnerable to the state would dare, nevertheless, to challenge it forcefully. Moral hazard offers a potential explanation of this important puzzle in certain cases, and thus may provide insight on how the international community can inhibit the escalation of internal conflict.

Although the recent phenomenon of *humanitarian* intervention can at best explain some escalation of internal conflict since the end of the Cold War, Crawford suggests that the moral hazard arising from a broader conception of intervention may explain earlier cases. For example, he cites Thucydides's explanation of the rebellions that accompanied the bipolar struggle between Athens and Sparta:

> The whole Hellenic world was convulsed, struggles being everywhere made by the popular chiefs to bring in the Athenians, and by the oligarchs to introduce the [Spartans]. . .With an alliance always at the command of either faction for the hurt of their adversaries and their own corresponding advantage, opportunities for bringing in the foreigner were never wanting to the revolutionary parties. . .. Revolution thus ran its course from city to city (1982, pp. 198–199).

He similarly notes that a prominent article of the 1990s observed that "hostile international environments spur internal conflict as outside states back rebel groups in enemy countries" (David, 1997, p. 554). What is fascinating about the putative moral hazard of humanitarian intervention after the Cold War is that it may explain why *benign* international environments likewise spur internal rebellion, which was not expected.

Crawford offers a typology of the ways in which the expectation of intervention may exacerbate internal conflict, distinguishing four types of moral hazard:

- *Acute*—if a specific threat of intervention triggers a rebellion in that state;
- *Chronic*—when a long-term history of intervention in a state perpetuates its instability;
- *Contagious*—if intervention in support of rebels in one state spurs rebellion in a neighbour;
- *Pervasive*—when an emerging norm of humanitarian intervention inadvertently encourages rebellions more broadly, as Kuperman has hypothesized.

These categories should be kept in mind to avoid unproductive debates that conflate distinct phenomena. Indeed, it is likely that scholars who downplay or dismiss one of these types of moral hazard will accept another. Each of the categories, moreover, suggests lines of inquiry that may contribute to distinct bodies of theory and research in international and comparative politics.

From a policy perspective debate centres on the following questions. Does humanitarian intervention, in individual cases or as an overall policy, exacerbate some ethnic violence? If so, how should this be weighed against the good it can do? And which reforms might reduce the harmful effect without undermining the beneficial one, thereby increasing intervention's net benefit? All the authors, with the possible exception of Western, acknowledge that expectations of outside intervention can exacerbate internal violence, by emboldening rebels and/or prompting states to attack preventively. Rauchhaus observes that any prospect of humanitarian intervention will increase rebels' expectations of the benefits of war and thereby promote provocative behaviour. Wagner likewise notes that, at least in theory, the most effective way to reduce internal war might be for the international community to re-embrace the norm of sovereignty that bars outside intervention in internal conflicts, although he acknowledges that this might be politically impossible. Kuperman analyses the difficulty of reducing the ill-effects of intervention without sacrificing life-saving benefits, and then offers two recommendations to optimize the net impact: stop intervening on behalf of rebels who provoke state retaliation against their own group; and, instead, raise pressure on states to meet the demands of non-violent groups. Although he acknowledges that the prescription may appear heartless and thus may be difficult to implement, he contends that it would save lives in the long run by discouraging rebellions that provoke genocidal retaliation, while still fostering gradual liberalization by oppressive governments.

The authors have not forged a consensus on the problem of moral hazard and intervention—nor on its solution. But, given the complexity and novelty of the theoretical and empirical claims at stake, it would be strange if we had. In lieu of consensus, this volume offers a range of methodologies, perspectives and prescriptions that highlight important questions for further research on the effects of intervention and the causes of civil war. We hope they will help shape debate about the costs, benefits and need for reform of the emerging norm of humanitarian intervention.

References

David, S. (1997) Internal war: causes and cures, *World Politics*, 49(4), pp. 552–576.
Thucydides (1982) *The Peloponnesian War* (New York: Random House).

Suicidal Rebellions and the Moral Hazard of Humanitarian Intervention

ALAN J. KUPERMAN

In the 1990s a burst of ethnic violence and the end of the Cold War gave rise to an emerging norm of humanitarian military intervention (Wheeler, 2004). US President Bill Clinton (1999) enunciated this doctrine clearly: "If the world community has the power to stop it, we ought to stop genocide and ethnic cleansing". Two years later the International Commission on Intervention and State Sovereignty (2001; Shue, 2004) went further by declaring a 'Responsibility to Protect', suggesting that failure to intervene by those capable of doing so would actually violate international law. More recently, in December 2004, a high-level UN panel reiterated: "We endorse the emerging norm that there is a collective international responsibility to protect, exercisable by the Security Council authorizing military intervention as a last resort, in the event of genocide and other large-scale killing, ethnic cleansing or serious violations of international humanitarian law" (United Nations, 2004).

The common wisdom underlying this emerging norm is that humanitarian military intervention reduces the amount of genocide and ethnic cleansing (forced migration), which together can be labelled 'genocidal violence'. However, this causal relationship has not been demonstrated, and there is some contrary empirical evidence and deductive

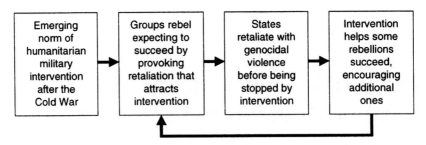

Figure 1. Moral hazard of humanitarian intervention and its potential consequences

logic suggesting that the intervention norm may at times actually cause genocidal violence. This is because the norm, intended as a type of insurance policy against genocidal violence, exhibits the pathology of all insurance systems by creating moral hazard that encourages risk-taking (see Figure 1). Specifically it encourages disgruntled sub-state groups to rebel because they expect intervention to protect them from genocidal retaliation by the state. Actual intervention, however, is often too late or feeble to prevent such retaliation. Thus, the norm causes some genocidal violence that otherwise would not occur. This chapter develops a theoretical framework to understand the problem; illustrates it in two cases; discusses analogous problems in economics; analyses potential remedies; and concludes by exploring the putative moral responsibility to intervene.

The Empirical Puzzle: Victim Groups Provoke Retaliation

The starting point for this exploration is a surprising, yet largely unexplored, empirical puzzle in the literature: most cases of genocidal violence arise when ethnic rebellions provoke massive state retaliation. ('Provoke' means to cause a reaction, whether intentionally or not.)[1] In other words, unlike in the prototypical case of genocide—the Nazi Holocaust against the Jews— most ethnic groups that fall victim to genocidal violence are responsible for initially militarizing the conflict. The obvious question is why would members of an ethnic group, which is sufficiently vulnerable to fall victim to genocidal violence at the hands of the state, provoke that very outcome by launching a suicidal rebellion against the state's authority? The puzzle is even more curious because the state typically issues advance warning to the ethnic group that it will respond to any such rebellion with massive retaliation.

Although counter-intuitive and little publicized, the finding that genocidal violence is usually provoked by members of the victim group is robust in the literature, across varying definitions, methodologies and timeframes within the post-World War II era, which is the only period for which reliable data are available. From 1943 to 1987 Harff and Gurr (1988) identify 44 episodes of 'genocide and politicide', defined as state-sponsored policies lasting for at least six months that deliberately kill thousands of non-combatants because of their identity or political affiliation, respectively (see Table 1).[2] They further divide the cases into six categories based on the motive of the perpetrator: hegemonic genocides aimed at forcing ethnic groups "to submit to central authority"; xenophobic genocides to promote "national protection or social purification"; repressive politicides in retaliation to "oppositional activity" by political parties; repressive/ hegemonic politicides also in retaliation to "oppositional activity" but in cases where

Table 1. Harff and Gurr's 44 cases of genocide and politicide from 1943 to 1987

Category	No.	Motive	No. in which killing was provoked by a violent challenge to the state's authority
Genocide			
Hegemonial	3	To force an ethnic group to submit to central authority	3 (by implication)
Xenophobic	3	To promote national protection or social purification	0
Politicide			
Repressive	15	In retaliation to acts of resistance by a political party	15 (by definition)
Repressive/ hegemonial	9	In retaliation to acts of resistance by an ethnic-based party	9 (by definition)
Retributive	4	Former opposition group takes revenge after seizing power	0
Revolutionary	10	By new regime against class or political enemies	3 (cross-listed as Repressive)
Total	44		30

the opposition party is ethnically based; retributive politicides by former opposition groups after seizing power to take revenge against former ruling groups; and revolutionary politicides by new regimes against "class or political enemies".

Harff and Gurr categorize 24 of the 44 cases (55%) as repressive or repressive/hegemonial, stating explicitly that the victim group "provokes this kind of mass murder" by "acts of resistance". Three other cases are categorized as hegemonial, which is closely related because the state's violence aims to force a communal group "to submit to central authority", which presupposes that the group is already resisting state authority. In addition, according to Harff and Gurr, three more cases tabulated as revolutionary can be categorized as repressive as well. Thus, based on Harff and Gurr's coding, at least 30 of the 44 cases (68%) exhibit the phenomenon in which rebels provoke their own group's demise by violently challenging the state's authority.[3]

In a separate research project Helen Fein (1990) focuses exclusively on genocide, ostensibly excluding cases of pure politicide in which victims did not share common ethnicity and were targeted solely for political reasons. This confines her database for the period 1945–88 to 19 cases, which she divides into four categories, also based on the motive of the perpetrator.[4] She uses different labels for categories that are quite similar to those of Harff and Gurr: their repressive category translates roughly into Fein's 'retributive'; revolutionary becomes 'ideological'; xenophobic becomes 'developmental'; and hegemonial becomes 'despotic'. Despite this semantic difference, Fein likewise finds that genocide is usually provoked by members of a group challenging the state: "one could classify at least 11 cases [58%] as retributive genocide in which the perpetrators retaliated to a real or perceived threat by the victim to the structure of domination". She also suggests that two of the other cases could be coded properly as retributive, which would raise the proportion in her database to 68% as well.[5]

For the post-cold war period I have compiled a database of large-scale, intrastate geno-cidal violence that has broken out since 1990, in which at least 50 000 non-combatants from an ethnic or political group were deliberately killed during a period in which at least 5000 were killed each year.[6] This comprises brief but intense campaigns, as well as sustained but less intense campaigns. It includes extermination campaigns that directly target civilians, war strategies that knowingly inflict collateral damage, and economic blockades or epi-sodes of ethnic cleansing that cause starvation and disease. However, it intentionally excludes cases of protracted low-level civilian killing typically arising from guerrilla or counter-insurgency campaigns, on the grounds that such violence is a qualitatively different phenomenon. It also avoids lumping together as a single case multiple incidents of mid-level violence that are separated by significant periods of relative calm.[7]

Based on available evidence, four cases from 1990–2004 clearly satisfy the definition above, as listed in Table 2.[8] Three of the four cases (75%)—Bosnia, Rwanda and Sudan (Darfur)—fit the pattern in which members of the victim group provoked the group's demise by violently rebelling. Burundi does not fit, because the ruling Tutsi perpetrated genocidal violence in response to a *peaceful* challenge to their authority, the election of the state's first Hutu president in 1993, rather than to a violent rebellion.[9]

The 'Rationality' of Genocidal Violence

Building on the literature's finding that most genocidal violence is provoked, many theor-ists agree that states act 'rationally' when they respond to such challenges with genocidal violence. ('Rational' action attempts to maximize one's interests based on available infor-mation and expectations.) Far from the popular caricature of genocidal violence as a psy-chopathic outburst, these theorists typically view such violence as a calculated action by the state to defend its power against an aggressive challenger. As Barbara Harff (1987) writes, "usually genocide is the conscious choice of policymakers ... for repressing (elimi-nating) opposition". Helen Fein (1979) long ago noted that "to grasp the origins of modern premeditated genocide, we must first recognize ... how it may be motivated or appear as a rational choice to the perpetrator". More recently, and more simply, Fein (1994) has con-cluded that genocide "is usually a rational act". Likewise, Roger W. Smith (1987) charac-terizes genocide as "a rational instrument to achieve an end". Peter du Preez (1994) says that

Table 2. Outbreaks of large-scale genocidal violence (including politicide) since 1990

Country	Perpetrator	Victim	Dates	Did victim group members provoke retaliation?
Bosnia	Serbs	Muslims	1992–95	Yes
Burundi	Tutsi	Hutu	1993–2000	No
Rwanda	Hutu	Tutsi	1994	Yes
Sudan	Arabs	Blacks in Darfur	2003–04	Yes
Total		4		3

Note: Nine other putative cases cannot yet be included because available evidence does not permit a determi-nation that a sufficient number of civilians of any group was killed deliberately. These cases are Afghanistan, Algeria, Democratic Republic of Congo, Iraq (vs Shiites), Liberia, North Korea, Russia (vs Chechens), Rwanda (vs Hutu) and Sierra Leone. In addition, three cases of genocidal violence during this period are excluded because they started before 1990: Angola, Somalia and Sudan (vs southerners).

genocidal violence is usually "perfectly rational" and even "pragmatic", because the state chooses this policy when "it is thought that mere military victory will not solve the problem and measures of 'population adjustment' are necessary".[10] Matthew Krain (1997) offers a similar rational explanation for state-sponsored mass murder: "elites trying to hold onto power can and must reconsolidate power quickly and efficiently". Going beyond these earlier theorists, who acknowledge but do not focus their scholarship on rational incentives, Benjamin Valentino (2000) emphasizes such perpetrator calculations and motivations as the core of his new "strategic" theory of "mass killing".

It is important to underscore that when theorists assert that a state pursues genocidal violence as a rational choice, it is not necessarily the optimal choice nor a moral one. When confronting rebellion, state leaders cannot be certain of the consequences of any policy alternative; in the absence of perfect information, rational action may be suboptimal.[11] Several policies may appear capable of achieving the interests of state leaders: offering concessions; pursuing counter-insurgency against armed elements; compelling forced migration; or attempting extermination. Nor is there yet conclusive case-study evidence that states typically do act rationally in this situation. Further research is needed to determine when and why states respond to rebellion with genocidal violence.

No Good Explanation of Suicidal Rebellions

In remarkable contrast to the chorus of rational explanations for perpetrator behaviour, there is no explicit rational theory to explain suicidal rebellions. Instead, theorists of genocidal violence imply that such rebellions are an all but inevitable response by vulnerable societal groups to long-term discrimination or oppression at the hands of the state. The literature thus harbours an implicit, non-rational theory for the phenomenon: vulnerable groups are driven by the frustration of prolonged discrimination to launch violent challenges against state authorities without necessarily calculating their chances of success or the consequences of failure, and thereby unwittingly provoke their own demise.

For example, Fein (1990) states that: "Domination by a ruling ethnoclass ... lead[s] to violent rebellion by the dominated class ... [provoking] expulsion and genocide". Likewise, Harff and Gurr (1989) write: "One tell-tale manifestation of conflicts with genocidal potential is discriminatory treatment of ethnic, religious, national, and regional minorities by dominant groups ... [Minorities] resisting discriminatory treatment are more likely to encounter massive state violence than quiescent groups." Despite the obvious risks of retaliation, say Harff and Gurr, discriminated groups pursue violent resistance because "leaders have alternatives, victims rarely do". But, in reality, discriminated groups almost always do have alternatives to violent resistance, which could enhance their welfare by reducing significantly their risk of suffering genocidal violence. The fact that Harff and Gurr view rebellion as all but inevitable, despite the availability of obvious, welfare-improving, alternative strategies, implies that they view subordinate group actions as irrational.

This implicit theory from the literature is depicted graphically by the bold arrows in Figure 2. Although it may account for much genocidal violence, it is under-specified at every juncture. First, the literature does not explain when and why states are dominated by certain groups that discriminate against others. Second, even if suffering discrimination were a necessary condition for a violent challenge against the state, which empirically is not true, such discrimination is clearly insufficient by itself because most groups suffering

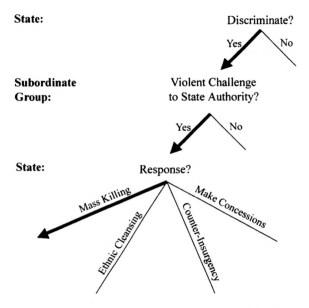

Figure 2. Tree of actions leading to most genocidal violence

discrimination do not launch such challenges.[12] Third, although genocidal violence may sometimes be a rational response by a state to such challenges, in other cases it may be equally or more rational for the state to concede to the demands of the challenging group, or to combat the challenge with a disciplined counter-insurgency aimed only at militants rather than at civilians. Thus the implicit theory is contingent at every turn on other factors ('condition variables') yet to be specified. Moreover, some cases of genocidal violence, such as the Holocaust, stem from an entirely different causal sequence.

This study seeks neither to redress all of these inadequacies in the literature, nor to formulate a new comprehensive theory of genocidal violence. Rather it seeks only to specify more fully the determinants of a key juncture along this most common path to genocidal violence: the decision by members of a vulnerable group to violently challenge the authority of a state, thereby provoking genocidal retaliation. Identifying the determinants of this decision could offer considerable insight into the causes of, and possible means of preventing, genocidal violence.

Why Men Rebel

Other scholars have explored the more general question of why people rebel or revolt.[13] However, their theories generally do not differentiate among rebellions that have greatly varying likelihood of success and cost of failure, so they are under-specified for the narrower phenomenon at issue in this study. In other words, low-cost, successful rebellions are much easier to explain than suicidal ones.

Nevertheless, the existing literature does offer insight into the causes and strategies of challenges to authority. For example, nearly all theorists cite perceived relative (rather than absolute) deprivation as the leading cause of revolution and rebellion, which can explain why such challenges are typically launched by groups that enjoy rising socioeconomic conditions. However, two underlying questions remain. First, 'relative' to whom or to what? Second, which factors mediate the connection to violence—that is, when does perceived relative deprivation actually lead to rebellion?

Aristotle (1971) wrote that people rebel "if they think that they have too little although they are the equals of those who have more". Marx focused on the relative material inequality between classes, predicting that workers would rebel even in the face of improving living standards if they perceived capitalist living standards to be rising even faster. Tocqueville crucially observed that relative deprivation alone is insufficient without an expectation that rebellion will improve the situation: "Evils which are patiently endured when they seem inevitable become intolerable when once the idea of escape from them is suggested". This explained his otherwise counter-intuitive empirical observation that revolution was more likely when states were relaxing, not intensifying, oppression.[14]

In the early 1960s James C. Davies (1971a) argued that the key relative deprivation is not between groups but rather between the expected and actual satisfaction of one group. Rebellion is caused by "an intolerable gap between what people want and what they get" and so is "most likely to occur when a prolonged period of objective economic and social development is followed by a short period of sharp reversal". Like Tocqueville, he identified the key mediating factor between deprivation and rebellion as the expectation of success. "It is when the chains have been loosened somewhat, so that they can be cast off without a high probability of losing life, that people are put in a condition of rebelliousness".[15]

But other theorists disagree about the impact of government repression on the likelihood of rebellion. David Schwartz (1971) and William Kornhauser (1964) argued in the early 1960s that rebellions arise when states crack down on peaceful reform movements, thereby leaving disgruntled constituents no alternative to violence.[16] In reality, government repression is a double edged-sword that can either staunch or provoke rebellion, depending on when and how it is used, which makes statistical correlation too blunt a methodology to provide useful insight.

Other theorists in the 1960s—including Lucian Pye, Edward Gude and Thomas Perry Thornton—identified the most decisive state policy as its reaction to initial acts of political violence. Indiscriminate retaliation backfires by mobilizing the population in favour of the rebellion out of sympathy and perceived self-defence. Rebel leaders are aware of this dynamic, Gude (1971) wrote, so that a key goal of their attacks is to "trigger governmental repression that can provide a basis for recruitment into an insurgent movement".[17] In other words, rebel leaders may initiate violence despite an unfavourable balance of forces in the hope that the government's over-reaction will aid rebel recruitment and thereby tilt the balance in their favour.

In the 1970s Charles Tilly (1978) and others focused on the general process of mobilization that is a precondition of rebellion. More recently theorists such as Doug McAdam (1982) and Sidney Tarrow (1994), echoing Tocqueville, have emphasized the mediating role of 'political opportunity structures' in determining when relative deprivation and mobilization actually lead to actions such as rebellions.

For more than three decades, Ted Robert Gurr has integrated the literature's findings into a general theory of ethno-cultural rebellion and political action. His primary causal variable remains relative deprivation, defined according to Davies as the difference between perceived entitlement and actual welfare, so that even relatively privileged groups may be motivated to rebel by perceived deprivation. Gurr claims three mediating variables determine whether this perception leads to group action: salience of ethnocultural identity, group capacity for mobilization (based partly on geography),[18] and political opportunities for success. All four variables have both domestic and international determinants. A final domestic political variable—whether state institutions and resources favour repression or accommodation of group demands—determines whether ethnopolitical action takes the form of peaceful protest or violent rebellion. Gurr concedes problems of endogeneity, noting the mutual causation between relative deprivation, salience of identity, and political mobilization.[19] In addition, Gurr sacrifices parsimony by specifying an additional 20 causal variables that underlie his five main ones.[20] Nevertheless, Gurr's theory remains useful as the most comprehensive inventory of variables and processes leading to rebellion and political protest.

Unfortunately, none of these theories resolves the puzzle of suicidal rebellions. They explain many things: how relative deprivation may motivate a group to want to change the status quo; how the salience of ethnic identity may intensify such feelings; how these factors and others may enable a group to mobilize; how the unavailability of institutions to redress grievances peacefully may lead to consideration of violent alternatives; how the expectation of success at low cost may induce a mobilized group to launch a rebellion; and what tactics of rebellion it may employ to maximize its chances. However, the literature does not explain why or when a group that is vulnerable to genocidal retaliation would launch a rebellion against a state that has explicitly threatened such punishment.

Rational Deterrence Theory for Intrastate Conflicts

This study adapts rational deterrence theory from international relations to comparative politics in order to explain the suicidal rebellions that provoke genocidal retaliation. In the ideal type the state is dominated by one ethnic group. This dominant group uses its control of the state to funnel itself resources and opportunities in employment, education, legal rights and infrastructure investments that are disproportionate to its share of the population and/or contribution to the economy. The dominant group discriminates against and may have disdain for subordinate groups. However, under ordinary circumstances, the dominant group does not engage in genocidal violence against them— despite having the ability to do so—because that would sacrifice the benefits of exploiting them and/or incur costs of fighting that are not justified by compensating benefits.

Subordinate groups, all things being equal, would prefer to change the status quo— either to be treated equally, to take control of the state themselves, to gain communal or regional autonomy, or to secede and take control of their own mini-state. Commonly, they pursue these goals peacefully, at little cost but small hope of success. They usually avoid launching rebellions against the state's authority because of a rational expectation of massive retaliation and failure. Thus subordinate groups are deterred from launching violent challenges, which in turn sustains the incentive of the dominant group not to commit genocidal violence against them. In this narrow sense, the status quo situation is mutually beneficial because both sides perceive themselves to be enjoying higher utility than if they were to engage each other in violence. Such convergence of interest is the hallmark of effective coercion, as Thomas Schelling (1966) long ago noted:

> Coercion by threat of damage also requires that our interests and our opponent's not be absolutely opposed. If his pain were our greatest delight and our satisfaction his greatest woe, we would just proceed to hurt and to frustrate each other. It is when his

pain gives us little or no satisfaction compared with what he can do for us, and the action or inaction that satisfies us costs him less than the pain we can cause, that there is room for coercion. Coercion requires finding a bargain, arranging for him to be better off doing what we want—worse off not doing what we want—when he takes the threatened penalty into account.

The key question, under this rational framework, is what changes in the mutually beneficial situation to make deterrence fail, so that a subordinate group launches a rebellion? Traditionally, rational deterrence theory posits that one state will defy a deterrent threat from another only when the expected utility of doing so outweighs that of acquiescing (Schelling, 1966). Translated to the domestic realm, the state can be viewed as attempting to deter groups from launching armed challenges by threatening massive retaliation. This version of the theory offers four possible explanations for the deterrence failure represented by rebellion. First, the state fails to communicate credible threats, so the group does not expect its rebellion to prompt genocidal retaliation. Second, the state fails to communicate credible reassurances, so the group expects to suffer genocidal violence regardless of whether it rebels. Third, the state communicates credible threats and reassurances, but the group expects to prevail—without the assistance of humanitarian intervention—at an acceptable cost in retaliation. Fourth, it is the prospect of humanitarian intervention—moral hazard--that leads the group to expect its rebellion to succeed at tolerable cost. Finally, the null hypothesis of 'irrational' action posits that such groups do not behave as unitary rational actors, so rebellion is not an attempt to maximize expected utility. Seemingly irrational action could be explained by many theories—including those of frustration-aggression[21] and bureaucratic politics[22]—but these would tend to be disproved by decisive evidence for any of the four rational hypotheses. (The five hypotheses are summarized in Table 3.)

Evidence from the Balkans

Two cases from the Balkans—Bosnia and Kosovo—illustrate how the moral hazard of humanitarian intervention has fostered suicidal rebellion since the end of the Cold War.[23] Bosnia, as noted in Table 2, is one of four clear-cut cases since 1990 where an armed challenge (here a 1992 secession led by the republic's Muslims) provoked large-scale genocidal retaliation. Kosovo's death toll was lower, but the dynamic was similar, as an ethnic Albanian rebellion in 1998–99 provoked retaliatory ethnic cleansing. The two cases provide an interesting variation in the dependent variable (rebellion) both within and between cases because the subordinate groups rebelled neither at first opportunity (in 1991) nor at the same time, while many other variables were held constant between the two cases, including the dominant group.

Table 3. Explanations for rebellion by groups vulnerable to genocidal retaliation

1	Don't perceive credible threat by state to retaliate
2	Expect victimization anyway, so nothing to lose
3	Expect victory at tolerable cost w/o intervention
4	Expect intervention to enable victory at tolerable cost
5	Don't behave as unitary rational actors

To demonstrate the decisive role of moral hazard, I evaluate all five explanations for rebellion in these two cases by process tracing (George, 1979; Van Evera, 1997) the decisions of the groups that eventually launched rebellions, based on interviews with at least a dozen senior officials of each. These officials include the eventual presidents of Bosnia and Kosovo, top rebel officers, clandestine weapons procurers, political party leaders and diplomats in charge of external relations. To mitigate a major concern in retrospective interview research—that officials may misrepresent history to make themselves look better[24]—their testimonies were cross-checked against contemporaneous journalistic accounts and interviews with political opponents.

In each case subordinate group officials came to favour rebellion because they expected that by provoking state retaliation they could attract humanitarian military intervention sufficient to achieve their goal of independence. Contending hypotheses fail: the groups were not blind to the dangers of rebellion; they believed they could avoid genocidal violence so long as they eschewed rebellion; they did not expect to prevail without outside intervention; and yet they did act rationally. They rebelled only when they believed that doing so would attract humanitarian military intervention sufficient to attain their political goals, and they decided in advance that genocidal retaliation was an acceptable cost of victory.

In Bosnia, before the outbreak of violence, Muslim leaders negotiated but then rejected two compromises that they acknowledge might have averted war and genocidal violence— either keeping the republic in a rump Yugoslavia or dividing it into ethnic cantons before secession. Instead, the Muslims organized and armed a 100 000-strong militia and (with the republic's Croats) declared Bosnia's independence in March 1992, against the will of Belgrade and the republic's Serbs, knowing this would trigger war and genocidal violence. As Bosnian President Alija Izetbegovic later admitted, "war could have been avoided if I accepted that Bosnia enters greater Serbia"—i.e. stayed within rump Yugoslavia. He also revealed why the Muslims pursued secession, despite knowing they could not defend against expected Serb retaliation: "Our tactics were to buy time . . . [pursuing] a zig-zag line for independence . . . so the international community would defend this country" (personal communication, 19 July 2000). His eventual foreign minister, Haris Silajdzic, confirms: "My main priority in the whole strategy was to get Western governments and especially the United States to get involved, because [Serbs] had the whole Army" (personal communication, 19 July 2000). Omer Behmen, perhaps the most influential Muslim official, also says the goal was to "put up a fight for long enough to bring in the international community" (personal communication, 12 October 1999).

The Muslims expected such intervention because, immediately after the Cold War, the international community started establishing a norm of humanitarian intervention by rescuing groups from aggression regardless of whether members of the group had provoked the violence. For example, when Kuwait defied Baghdad's demand to halt alleged theft of Iraqi oil, Saddam Hussein invaded in August 1990, but a UN coalition expelled Iraqi troops and restored Kuwait's sovereignty, as US President George H. W. Bush declared a 'new world order'. When Iraq's Kurds rebelled soon after, the USA intervened in April 1991, protecting them from genocidal retaliation and facilitating their long-sought goal of political autonomy. When Croatia seceded from Yugoslavia in June 1991, triggering retaliation from local Serb and Yugoslav forces, the UN deployed a peacekeeping force (based in the Bosnian capital of Sarajevo, no less) that maintained a ceasefire, facilitated aid and protected Croatia's sovereignty. This emerging norm encouraged Bosnia's Muslims to believe that they too could benefit from international intervention to gain independence for a unitary Bosnian state by arming and seceding from Yugoslavia, despite the massive military superiority of the Serbs. This expectation was strongly reinforced in March 1992, shortly before the secession, when the USA and the European Community indicated that they would recognize a Bosnian declaration of independence despite vociferous Serb opposition.

Even after the Serbs' initial genocidal retaliation to the secession failed to prompt decisive intervention on behalf of the Muslims, the latter continued to fight a losing war in the hope of eventually garnering sufficient international military assistance to prevail (Burg & Shoup, 1999). The commander of UN peacekeepers, General Michael Rose (1998), reports that the weaker, Muslim side repeatedly rejected ceasefires, based on an expectation that if they "attacked and lost, the resulting images of war and suffering guaranteed support in the West for the 'victim State'". Even James Gow (1997), overtly sympathetic to the Muslims, concedes that their army broke ceasefires "in the hope of provoking a US intervention".

Ultimately this Muslim strategy did attract intervention: the USA facilitated the provision of weapons to the Muslims and their Croat allies and then led a NATO bombing campaign against Serb military assets. The intervention was too weak, however, to deliver the Muslims' goal of a unitary Bosnia immediately, and in 1995 at Dayton they had to settle for an ethnic division of the republic similar to that they had rejected in favour of war. The cost of three years of war was roughly two million displaced and 150 000 dead, mostly Muslim. Had it not been for the expectation of international intervention, the Muslims might not have seceded at all, or at least not without first agreeing to a cantonization plan, so the bloody Bosnian war might have been averted. At the very least, without the moral hazard created by the prospect of intervention, the Muslims would have militarily prepared themselves better before declaring independence, and thereby mitigated any potential genocidal retaliation.

In Kosovo, similarly, there was no genocidal violence until the province's ethnic Albanians launched a rebellion in 1998. Although Serbia had revoked Kosovo's autonomy in 1989, citing Albanian nationalism and discrimination against Serbs, and the Albanians responded by boycotting government institutions, there was virtually no deadly violence—and certainly no ethnic cleansing or genocide—for eight years while the Albanians embraced passive resistance. Indeed, by establishing parallel institutions for education, health care and taxes, the Albanians succeeded at restoring a degree of *de facto* autonomy. The peace was broken only when Albanians of the Kosovo Liberation Army (KLA) launched a full-blown rebellion in 1998, aiming to provoke state retaliation that would attract humanitarian military intervention sufficient to achieve independence. The rebels rejected pacifism on grounds that only a militant strategy could attract the intervention necessary for independence, based on the precedents of Bosnia and Croatia.

Belgrade initially responded with a brutal counter-insurgency that defeated the rebels but displaced tens of thousands of Albanian civilians. In autumn 1998, however, the USA threatened to intervene militarily on humanitarian grounds, which compelled Serbian forces to retreat and enabled the rebels to regroup, thereby renewing the war. In March 1999 Belgrade rejected a US-dictated peace plan at Rambouillet and NATO announced that it would bomb Serbia. Belgrade countered by forcibly expelling about 850 000 Albanians—half their total in Kosovo—in less than a month, while killing another 10 000. After 11 weeks of bombing, Belgrade capitulated, whereupon the Albanian refugees returned and forcibly expelled about 100 000 Serbs—likewise half their total in the province—in just a few weeks, while killing hundreds more.

The KLA rebellion was facilitated by the sudden availability of small arms arising from a civil war in neighbouring Albania in 1997, but the rebels never expected these light weapons to enable them to defeat the better equipped and larger Serbian army. As admitted by a top KLA commander, Emrush Xhemajli, "We knew our attacks would not have any military value. Our goal was not to destroy the Serb military force [but to make it] become more vicious ... We thought it was essential to get international support to win the war" (personal communication, 9 August 2000). Likewise, an Albanian negotiator at Rambouillet, Dugi Gorani, admits that "The more civilians were killed, the chances of international intervention became bigger, and the KLA of course realized that". The rebels anticipated and accepted the human cost of their strategy. Hashim Thaci, a founder of the KLA and head of its political directorate during the war, concedes: "We knew full well that any armed action we undertook would trigger a ruthless retaliation by Serbs against our people ... We knew we were endangering civilian lives, too, a great number of lives" (Little, 2000a; 2000b).

The rebels expected to benefit from humanitarian intervention even if they provoked the violence because of precedents and signals from the international community. They revealed in a May 1998 press report their intention to "attract heavy Yugoslav barrages and thus win strong international sympathy, as the Croats did in Vukovar" (Loza, 1998). A leading Kosovo Albanian journalist similarly noted: "There is a message that is being sent to the Kosovars—if you want to draw international attention you have to fight for it. That is exactly it. You need to use violence to achieve your goals." Gorani subsequently revealed that "there was this foreign diplomat who once told me, 'Look unless you pass the quota of five thousand deaths you'll never have anybody permanently present in Kosovo from the foreign diplomacy'" (Little, 2000b).[25]

Because the KLA strategy was based entirely on attracting humanitarian intervention and the rebels harboured no hope of prevailing themselves, violence could well have been averted if not for the moral hazard of humanitarian intervention. As Diana Johnstone (1998) noted: "without the prospect of decisive outside intervention on their behalf, the ethnic Albanians of Kosovo might have tried to make use of the existing legal framework" in Yugoslavia to restore autonomy, rather than violently seeking independence. Even after the outbreak of violence, if the international community had eschewed intervention, Belgrade could have snuffed out the rebellion at the cost of a few hundred lives, mostly rebels, as it appeared to have done by mid-1998. Instead, Western threats and bombing caused the violence to mushroom, leading to 10 000 deaths and the ethnic cleansing of nearly a million Albanians and Serbs—a perverse consequence indeed for an emerging norm of 'humanitarian' intervention.

Obviously, the moral hazard of humanitarian intervention cannot explain all rebellion that triggers genocidal retaliation, because the emerging norm is largely a post-cold war phenomenon, while such violence is timeless.[26] Nevertheless, these cases demonstrate that moral hazard has helped to cause genocidal violence in at least two recent instances. It is thus worthwhile to explore whether and how such moral hazard can be mitigated.

Lessons about Moral Hazard from Economics

The concept of moral hazard is examined most thoroughly in the literature of economics. A typical example is when a government provides deposit insurance to ensure depositors of the safety of their savings accounts in the event of a bank failure. The goal is to promote the stability of the banking system and the larger economy by promoting savings and thereby investment. However, one consequence of insuring depositors against bank losses is that they are less careful about which bank they choose, so long as it is insured. As depositors become less careful about scrutinizing banks, the banks themselves become less careful about the loans they make, especially given that the government will bail them out in the event of losses. This leads to more bad loans and bank failures, both of which are bad for the economy. Thus a policy intended to improve the economy by insuring against risk can have the unintended consequence of hurting the economy.

This domestic example of economic moral hazard has been replicated on an international scale in recent years by the advent of bail-outs from the International Monetary Fund (IMF). Such bail-outs provide an infusion of hard currency to states in emerging markets that otherwise would default on their foreign debt because of severe balance of payments deficits. The goal is to preserve the economic stability of such states and the international system by reassuring lenders and investors that they can continue to do business in emerging markets without fear of huge losses. However, by reducing the penalty to states for risky economic policies and to lenders for risky loans, the policy of bail-outs has the unintended consequence of encouraging these inefficient behaviours that undermine economic stability.[27]

To reduce moral hazard, a common prescription is to restrict insurance only to those who abide by regulations. In the domestic context the government provides deposit insurance only to those banks that pay a small premium and follow strict rules about the type and amount of loans they make relative to their deposits. In the international context the IMF provides bail-outs only to those states that agree to undergo structural adjustment— modifying their economic policies in ways that reduce the likelihood of future balance of payments deficits.

Although such regulatory schemes can mitigate moral hazard, it is important to recognize that there is generally an inverse relationship between moral hazard and risk, such that regulators cannot eliminate both. If regulators reduce moral hazard by setting stringent qualification requirements for insurance or bail-outs, most banks or states will fail to qualify and the system will have almost as much risk for depositors and lenders as if there were no insurance or bail-outs. If regulators reduce this risk by setting lower qualification requirements, moral hazard grows, as states and banks feel free to engage in irresponsible practices. Put another way, regulators cannot simultaneously reduce both the expected cost of taking risks and the propensity to take such risks.

Regulation of moral hazard in domestic banking also poses two further dangers. If regulatory requirements are set too low, there may be so much risky behaviour and so many bail-outs that the insurance system is bankrupted. Alternatively, if regulatory requirements are set too high, banks will not be permitted to make sufficient loans, and overall economic growth may be strangled.

The optimum solution is the regulatory sweet spot, which balances reasonable levels of moral hazard against risk, and which promotes liquidity while avoiding insolvency of the insurance system. Even if these challenges can be surmounted, however, there is a final obstacle to limiting moral hazard, which stems from the fact that the regulator and regulated are involved in a game of chicken. The regulator threatens to deny insurance unless the regulated abides by strict regulations. But the regulated knows that the regulator wants to provide insurance for its own reasons, so the threat lacks credibility and the regulated may feel free to ignore the regulations.

For example, in the domestic context, the government does not want any depositor to lose money when a bank fails, because that could hurt the confidence of other depositors and thereby damage the economy. Accordingly, the government may provide protection to depositors even at uninsured banks and/or provide protection above the statutory limit at insured banks. In the USA, even though deposit insurance is limited to $100 000 per depositor at each bank, when a failure occurs the government routinely bails out all accounts (according to the 'too big to fail' doctrine). This policy seeks to reduce the risk to depositors so as to prevent a run on banks, but unintentionally also increases moral hazard. Banks and depositors, expecting they will be bailed out fully in any circumstance, are more prone to engage in risky behaviour. Analogously, a state in fiscal crisis knows that the IMF does not want it to default because of the danger of international contagion, which reduces the credibility of the IMF's threat to withhold a bail-out in the absence of economic reform. Because such states expect to be bailed out in any case, they often violate pledges of structural adjustment by continuing inefficient economic policies to obtain short-term domestic political gains.

Applying the Lessons from Economics

All these problems of moral hazard apply to humanitarian intervention as well (see Table 4). The international community has sought to insure vulnerable groups against the risk of genocidal violence by establishing an emerging norm of humanitarian military intervention. In so doing, however, it has inadvertently encouraged such groups to engage in the risky behaviour of launching rebellions that may provoke genocidal retaliation. (A distinction can be drawn between a group that intentionally provokes genocidal retaliation and one that knowingly runs a high risk of provoking such retaliation. The distinction is not theoretically significant, however, so long as both groups expect to fail without intervention, expect to succeed if their rebellion provokes retaliation because that will attract humanitarian intervention, and accept in advance that genocidal retaliation is a tolerable cost to achieve their political goal.) The emerging norm creates moral hazard even though it does not absolutely guarantee intervention, just as the prospect of IMF bailouts creates moral hazard despite likewise being only probabilistic.

In theory the international community could attempt to reduce moral hazard by setting strict regulatory requirements for its 'insurance'—for example, pledging not to intervene on behalf of groups that provoke retaliation by rebelling. This could deter groups from rebelling, and thereby prevent much genocidal violence. On the other hand, this policy might increase the suffering of some groups by denying them intervention if they rebelled anyway. Another deleterious effect could be to prolong the oppression of some groups by inhibiting their liberation via rebellion, thereby hindering the liberal international goal of democratization. (This is analogous to a banking regulator establishing overly strict loan requirements that choke off economic growth.) But this problem could be offset at least partially if the international community also provided greater support to pacifist liberation movements by pressuring and enticing states to appease them.

An alternative strategy to reduce genocidal violence would be to lower regulatory requirements, pledging to intervene on behalf of any group that faced genocide or ethnic cleansing, which is the logical endpoint of the emerging norm. However, this would increase moral hazard and thus tend to raise the incidence of rebellions that provoke genocidal retaliation. Unless such a policy deterred retaliation more than it

Table 4. Comparing moral hazard in economics and ethnic conflict

	Banking	IMF	Ethnic conflict
Goal	Prevent lost deposits and bolster economy	Prevent suffering and promote global growth	Stop and deter genocidal violence
Safety net	Deposit insurance	Bail-outs	Humanitarian military intervention
Primary risky behaviour promoted	Risky loans by banks	BOP and fiscal deficits in emerging market states	Rebellions
Secondary risky behaviour promoted	Deposits in weak banks	International loans to profligate states	International support for demands by militants
Negative consequence	More bank failures	More defaults	More genocidal violence
Regulation to mitigate moral hazard	Reserve requirements	Structural adjustment conditionality	No intervention if rebels provoke retaliation
Two dangers from strict regulation . . .			
If standard not met	Most deposits are at risk	Few bail-outs, so states default	Some genocidal retaliation permitted
If standard met	Few loans, so economy contracts	Austerity hurts the poor and inhibits growth	Some discrimination and oppression continues
Danger from lax regulation	FDIC bankrupted	IMF bankrupted	Intervention resources exhausted
'Chicken' undermines regulators' credibility	Too big to fail	Avoiding contagion	CNN effect

promoted rebellions, it could increase genocidal violence sufficiently to exhaust the intervention resources of the international community. This would be analogous to the bankruptcy of a deposit insurance system, but with even starker human consequences.

As in economics, regulators of humanitarian intervention also have problems convincing the regulated that their threats are credible. In Kosovo Western officials repeatedly attempted to deter the Albanians from escalating their rebellion by declaring that NATO would not be the "air force of the KLA" (Matthews, 1998; Samyn, 1998; Brown, 1998; Cornwell, 1999; Wintour, 1999; Matthews & Bowman, 1999). However, the rebels calculated that, if they could provoke Serb retaliation against Albanian civilians, the West would be compelled by media coverage of the humanitarian tragedy (the 'CNN effect') to intervene despite its declarations. Western threats to withhold intervention were not credible and thus could not deter the KLA from engaging in risky behaviour (Crawford, 2003).

However, moral hazard in humanitarian intervention is different from that in some economic models in at least two respects. First, the value of a bail-out may be greater than the value of responsible behaviour. Thus we observe the bizarre dynamic in which the insured group sometimes engages in risky behaviour to intentionally provoke its own suffering, in order to garner a bail-out. One cannot imagine a depositor searching for the worst bank possible so as to lose his money in order to get a government bail-out, because the bail-out has a value no greater than that of a responsible investment, which can be found fairly easily. By contrast, in domestic power struggles, vulnerable groups may expect that if they provoke state retaliation, humanitarian intervention will not only protect them but will also enable them to achieve otherwise unattainable political goals such as independence. Thus, while both humanitarian intervention policies and well designed insurance policies reduce the costs to actors of risky behaviour, only the former actually rewards actors for such behaviour, encouraging even greater risks. This is because, unlike insurance systems, the emerging norm of humanitarian intervention is unregulated against fraudulent claims.

Some insurance systems exhibit a similar problem if fraud can be committed with impunity. For example, if a building depreciates below the value of its fire insurance policy, the policy holder has a perverse incentive to commit arson, so long as he expects this criminal fraud not to be detected and punished. Another example is in unemployment insurance. If a worker in the official economy knows he can take a job at a slightly lower wage in the unofficial economy, he may have an incentive to provoke his boss to fire him, so he can collect both unemployment compensation and the income from the black-market job, which together exceed his regular wage. Again, this perverse incentive exists only if the worker expects that such fraudulent behaviour can be committed without detection, which would curtail the unemployment compensation and thus reduce net income. The difference in humanitarian intervention is that such fraudulent abuse of the insurance system—provoking genocidal retaliation against one's own group to attract intervention—is not necessarily punished by loss of insurance even when detected, because the international community may still intervene to help the provocateur group.

Another difference in the realm of ethnic conflict is that the potential punishment (genocidal retaliation) for risky behaviour (rebellion) is more clearly the result of human agency than the 'invisible hand' of economic forces. Thus it is theoretically possible for a humanitarian intervention norm to deter states from engaging in genocidal retaliation against rebellious groups. This deterrent effect requires intervention threats to be clear, credible, sizeable and accompanied by credible reassurances of non-intervention if states eschew genocidal violence. In practice, however, humanitarian intervention has been inconsistent, and often belated and inadequate as well, thereby reducing its deterrent effect. Nonetheless, even such a sub-optimal intervention norm may deter some retaliation, thereby mitigating the violence arising from moral hazard. Only empirical study can determine whether the net effect of the emerging norm of humanitarian intervention is to increase or decrease genocidal violence.

Prescriptions for the Real World

The cases and analysis suggest a number of prescriptions to mitigate genocidal violence, but they all face practical hurdles to implementation. A common suggestion by humanitarian advocates is to intervene quickly in all cases of genocidal violence so as to physically curtail its extent in the short run and deter its incidence in the long run. But this is impossible given the current global capacity for intervention. The 1990s alone witnessed major civil violence in at least 16 areas, some on multiple occasions: Albania, Algeria, Angola, Azerbaijan, Bosnia, Cambodia, Congo Republic, Croatia, Ethiopia, Liberia, Kosovo, Sierra Leone, Somalia, Sudan, Tajikistan and Zaire. Intervening in all of them would have required simultaneous deployment of hundreds of thousands of troops—well beyond the world's capacity to project force.[28] Moreover, by the logic of moral hazard, each intervention raises expectations of future ones, thereby encouraging additional rebellions that may provoke genocidal retaliation and further overwhelm intervention resources.[29]

The opposite strategy is to inhibit the rebellions that provoke genocidal retaliation. One option is to block militants' access to weapons because, as Kosovo demonstrated for nearly a decade, an unarmed challenge to authority is far less likely to provoke such retaliation. Unfortunately, global proliferation of light arms and the porous nature of international borders makes this option generally impractical.

Another way to inhibit rebellion is to reduce moral hazard by explicitly denying intervention to groups that provoke genocidal retaliation. Such a strategy is not without shortcomings. As noted, if it worked by deterring rebellion, it could prolong the oppression faced by some groups. But the international community could employ other means to entice states to reduce oppression. Moreover, Bosnia demonstrates that some armed challenges are launched by groups who face no discrimination—and there is little downside to deterring that.

The bigger problem arises from the risk that groups would doubt the policy's credibility and launch rebellions anyway, expecting media images of suffering to compel intervention. Only if the international community could muster the discipline to resist intervening in the first few cases might it build sufficient credibility to deter further rebellions. But, given the pluralism of the international system, the democratic nature of most states, the multiple grounds for and means of intervention and the expansion of world-wide media coverage, it is unclear if the global community could refuse repeatedly to intervene in such cases. Thus, one possible outcome of such a declared policy would be intermittent intervention that would create some moral hazard and fail to protect some victims of genocidal retaliation—not entirely different from the current reality.

Another option to reduce moral hazard—in cases where a group has legitimate grievances and is led by a pacifist leader, such as the Kosovo Albanians under Ibrahim Rugova from 1989–98—is for the international community to bolster this leader and hinder the emergence of militant rivals by enticing or coercing the state to appease the group. Unfortunately, the international community has demonstrated a lack of will to devote large resources until cases turn violent. This stubborn pattern has the effect of rewarding militants at the expense of pacifists, thereby promoting rebellion that spurs genocidal retaliation.

A final prescription is to better coordinate military intervention with coercive diplomacy (Kuperman, 1996; 1999; 2004c). Since the Cold War the international community has repeatedly attempted to coerce authoritarian governments to hand over power to opponents by applying economic or military sanctions. In Kosovo NATO threatened to and did bomb Yugoslavia to force it to accept agreements designed to achieve the province's independence. In Bosnia the USA and European Community backed the republic's secession and pressured Belgrade to accept it. In both cases the attempted coercion backfired when the state opted to kill or ethnically cleanse its opponents rather than hand power to them. This pattern also played out in Rwanda and East Timor.

To protect against such backlash, the international community would have to deploy robust intervention forces preventively, before exercising coercive diplomacy. So far, however, preventive deployments have been feeble. When violence breaks out, as in Rwanda or Srebrenica, peacekeepers provide little protection and then are withdrawn, leaving the targeted groups to suffer their fate. Such half-hearted deployments create their own moral hazard, lending a false sense of security that leads vulnerable groups to lower their guard so that they ultimately die in greater numbers—which makes this type of intervention worse than nothing.

If the international community is unwilling to deploy robust forces preventively, it should temper its use of coercive diplomacy aimed at compelling rulers to surrender power, because of the risk of inadvertently triggering genocidal violence against domestic opponents. Diplomats should focus on carrots rather than sticks—offering oppressive governments incentives, including economic assistance, in exchange for gradual power sharing. The international community also should be prepared to offer 'golden parachutes'—monetary rewards, asylum and immunity from subsequent prosecution—to entrenched dictators willing to hand over power peacefully. While human rights groups abjure the prospect of cutting deals with leaders who have blood on their hands, in some cases forgiving past crimes may be the price of preventing future ones.

In the wake of the terror attacks of 11 September 2001 the international community, especially the USA, has switched its military focus from altruistic humanitarian intervention to a self-interested war against terrorism and proliferation. One unintended benefit may be that disgruntled groups are now less likely to provoke genocidal retaliation in the expectation of attracting humanitarian intervention. They know that in today's environment the USA is more likely to view such rebels as terrorists and therefore to support state retaliation against them. This may help explain why nascent rebellions by Albanian rebels in Macedonia and southern Serbia have fizzled out, at least for now, rather than replicating the dynamics of Bosnia and Kosovo. However, the Sudanese case of Darfur, where black Muslim groups in 2003 launched a rebellion that had no hope of military success but did provoke genocidal retaliation leading to calls for intervention, suggests that the dynamic persists (Dealey, 2004; Kuperman, 2004b).

A 'Moral Responsibility' to Intervene?

Since the end of the Cold War the emerging norm has asserted not merely an international right but also a responsibility to intervene militarily to prevent genocidal violence.[30] However, regardless of whether one believes in a general cosmopolitan responsibility to groups outside one's own border, most observers would agree that the primary responsibility for protecting a group rests with the group itself and, by delegation, with its leaders. Accordingly, if a group's leaders wilfully choose to sacrifice their own civilians by rebelling, as a means to an end, it is not obvious that the international community automatically has a responsibility to protect those civilians by intervening.

In light of the controversial and counter-intuitive nature of this concept—the absence of a naturally occurring moral responsibility to intervene in cases of genocidal violence—it is useful to illustrate the point with a thought experiment. As is well known, most states around the world exhibit some form of domestic discrimination, whether against women, ethnic groups, castes or some other subordinate group—in most cases without any significant level of overt violence. Few observers would argue that there is a generalized right or responsibility of the international community to intervene with military force in the internal affairs of states to rectify such domestic inequality. Accordingly, the status quo in much of the world is structural inequality, accompanied by a widespread consensus that the international community has no right or responsibility to use military force to improve the lot of subordinate groups. The question is, what happens when members of a subordinate group start shooting government authorities and civilians of the dominant group, thereby provoking retaliation? Does such violence by a subordinate group suddenly create a new right or responsibility of the international community to intervene with military force on its behalf? In other words, if the subordinate group was not entitled to such intervention previously, can it possibly 'earn' such an entitlement through the act of killing people? If the group cannot earn a new right by committing violence, the international community continues to have no inherent responsibility to intervene. This is especially true if, as in most cases, the group can end the retaliation itself without intervention by simply halting its rebellion.

Nevertheless, four circumstances can be envisioned in which the international community might have a responsibility to intervene to protect subordinate groups. One possibility is if the state attacks a subordinate group in the absence of any violent provocation. In such a case, the group cannot protect itself through passivity, so the international community might have a responsibility to protect it. As noted above, however, this scenario is atypical because most genocidal violence is provoked by rebellion.

A second possibility is if rebels act without the support of most members of their group. Here again most of the group cannot protect itself by halting the rebellion, so the international community might have a responsibility to intervene. This argument applies to cases such as Kosovo, where the rebellion was launched by KLA militants without the support of most of the province's Albanians. But it would not apply in Bosnia, where an overwhelming majority of the Muslim populace voted both to elect their secessionist leaders and to approve the referendum on independence, despite vocal Serb opposition and threats of retaliation.

A third possibility is if leaders of a group withhold information from the group in order to obtain its support for rebellion. In such a case group members may lack sufficient information to evaluate the consequences of various policies and thereby to protect themselves, so the international community might have a responsibility. This conceivably was the case in Bosnia, where the Muslim populace may have been less aware than its leadership that a unilateral declaration of independence was likely to provoke genocidal retaliation. However, the lack of perfect information is a pervasive situation in life, not usually held to erase responsibility for one's actions. Thus it is not clear that a subordinate group's lack of perfect information relieves it of the primary responsibility to protect itself.

A final possibility is if a group rebels based on promises made, or expectations raised, by the international community. Only in such a case would the international community have a clear and unambiguous responsibility to protect the group. For example, if a group rebelled because of expectations created by the emerging norm of humanitarian intervention, the international community would have a responsibility to protect the group from retaliation. This underscores, however, that the responsibility is not inherent but stems from the international community's choices in establishing norms.[31] In other words, the international community does not have a clear responsibility to intervene unless it adopts a policy of intervening.

Accordingly, intervention policy cannot and should not be dictated by any purported, inherent responsibility to intervene in all cases of genocidal violence. Intervention policy is precisely that: a question of policy, not merely of morality. Although it is not obvious what the goal of that policy should be, one obvious choice is to try to reduce the overall incidence of genocidal violence. If such a goal were chosen, the optimum policy would be determined not by good intentions or the automatic embrace of imagined responsibilities but by the real-world consequences, intended and otherwise, of that policy.

Conclusion: Balancing Competing Values

The stated goal of the emerging norm of humanitarian intervention is to reduce genocidal violence. However, reducing violence is not the sole human value, nor always the predominant one. One can envision arguments that intervention policy should promote other values, such as freedom or democracy, even at the expense of increased violence.

Similar debates pervade the literature on moral hazard. Economists generally advocate designing insurance to be 'market neutral', so the insured will act as they would in the absence of insurance. But others claim this ignores positive externalities of the risk-prone behaviour that is encouraged by moral hazard. For example, although health insurance indisputably encourages excessive use of medical services, some health-care advocates consider this preferable to what they consider the under-utilization of such services in the absence of insurance (Nyman, 2001). Likewise, although unemployment insurance and welfare benefits encourage some laziness and fraud, advocates view this cost as outweighed by the social benefit of helping the truly needy (Baker, 1996).

To design insurance that optimally promotes society's values, it is essential that these values be debated openly. Unfortunately, this has not yet occurred in either the popular or the academic literature on humanitarian intervention. Some supporters of intervention appear to favour humanitarian intervention even if it encourages rebellion that provokes genocidal retaliation, because they place higher value on what they perceive to be the liberation agenda of the rebels. However, intervention proponents rarely make this case publicly. Instead, they rely on the empirically false but widely accepted assumption that intervention can do only good. They commonly also claim that any rebellion that provokes genocidal retaliation must *ipso facto* be a liberation movement, based on the horrific response of the state—but this does not follow logically.

Such supporters of military intervention for purposes of liberation should make their case explicitly, rather than cloaking their advocacy in the garb of humanitarian intervention, which confuses both debates. If such liberal hawks, or hawkish liberals, prize freedom over human life, they should have the courage to say so openly and see whether society at large supports them or not.

The alternative to a policy of intervening militarily on the side of rebels who claim to be pursuing liberation is not necessarily to doom their peoples to perpetual oppression. Some of these groups, such as Bosnia's Muslims, faced no oppression or violence until they acquired weapons and challenged state authority. In such cases it is rebellion that causes oppression, not vice versa. More generally, an alternative to aiding rebels is to utilize international leverage to compel states to address the legitimate grievances of non-violent groups. While such a policy might not produce the quick results or visceral satisfaction of helping rebels militarily defeat a perceived oppressor, it could avoid provoking genocidal retaliation against innocent civilians. Ultimately, that is the choice the international community may face: whether to foster revolutionary change at the cost of genocidal violence or to settle for more gradual progress at a substantially lower human toll. It is a debate worth having—on these terms explicitly.

Notes

The original version of this study was presented at the annual meeting of the International Studies Association, Chicago, IL, 21–24 February 2001. Revised versions have been presented at more than a dozen international conferences and university seminars. The author would like to thank all those who offered comments, particularly Barry Posen for his early guidance and Timothy Crawford for his close reading of the penultimate version.

1. In both the Webster's and American Heritage dictionaries, only one of four definitions includes intentionality.
2. Subsequently Harff (1994) broadened these definitions to include policies sponsored by non-state actors in the case of civil war. For a critique of their methods, see Fein (1990). In addition to disputing their broad definition, she notes that, by counting each case by perpetrator rather than victim, they lump together several cases in the USSR and Iran.
3. Some of the other cases in Harff and Gurr's database would also satisfy this definition if re-coded properly. For example, the authors erroneously categorize the killing of Tutsi in Rwanda in 1963–64 as retributive on the grounds that it was perpetrated by new Hutu leaders in retaliation for years of Tutsi oppression. In fact, such retributive violence ended in Rwanda soon after the Hutu seized power in 1959. The subsequent killing of 1963–64 was rather a response by the Hutu nationalist state to fresh challenges to its authority from invading Tutsi refugee rebels and their domestic Tutsi allies—a fairly typical case of repressive politicide. Accordingly, 68% may represent a conservative (i.e. low-end) estimate of the proportion of cases from 1943–87 in which the ultimate victim group provoked its own demise, based on Harff and Gurr's database.
4. Fein operationalizes this distinction not on the basis of any objective definition, but rather by selecting cases identified as genocide by at least two of three prominent expert studies. The experts she relies on are Ezell, Kuper, and Harff and Gurr. In a subsequent study, Fein (1993) identifies only 16 cases during the same period without acknowledging or explaining the discrepancy with her earlier study. In the latter study she also distinguishes genocide from "genocidal massacres" or "pogroms", which are briefer or more episodic, and from "mass political killings", a term she does not define clearly but which appears to refer to killings of civilians during civil wars. It is not clear if she operationalizes these distinctions by rigorous standards.
5. She is not absolutely precise about which cases are retributive. However, she does identify seven cases precisely as ideological, developmental or despotic, which leaves 12 rather than 11 cases as retributive. In addition, she says that one of the cases identified as despotic, Uganda, included periods of retributive genocide, which potentially raises the number of retributive cases to 13.
6. I include the targeting of political groups, even though this category of victim was excluded from the UN convention's definition of genocide under pressure from member states including the USSR. Other authors have chosen to coin new terms to indicate such a broader definition—for example, "mass killing" in Valentino (2004) and "democide" in Rummel (1992).
7. The quantitative thresholds of 50 000 total and 5000 annually are arbitrary. As with any such arbitrary definition, cases that fall marginally short of the standard could probably be included in the universe without significantly affecting its characteristics. Furthermore, an argument could be made for utilizing an alternative threshold based on the percentage, rather than absolute toll, of people killed within the victim group. However, this alternative would have two drawbacks. First, it could include some cases with relatively low death tolls (in cases where the target group was small), while excluding others with significantly higher death tolls (among big target groups). Second, determining the size of the target population in many cases would be subjective, because it could depend on whether an entire ethnic group were counted or only that portion within a state or region. While my definition is arbitrary, it does have the merit of being relatively objective, at least to the extent that existing death-count estimates are. It is possible that my high threshold may exclude some less violent examples of the very phenomenon I seek to examine, but that is the unavoidable price of seeking to exclude different phenomena such as terrorism or counterinsurgency campaigns that generally have lower death tolls. I accept this trade-off consciously, preferring to ensure that all cases in my universe represent the same phenomenon, rather than that the universe contain all examples of the phenomenon.
8. Darfur in the Sudan is too recent to be listed in published databases. The other three cases are the only ones that satisfy my definition in a prominent database of genocides and politicides perpetrated prior to 2002, in Harff (2003).

9. Despite the peaceful nature of the challenge, hardline Tutsi feared that peaceful Hutu consolidation of political power would lead to violence against them or threats to their way of life, and so they assassinated the new Hutu president and reclaimed power in 1993, triggering mutual ethnic violence and a Hutu rebel insurgency. The new Tutsi government then responded to the Hutu insurgency with a seven-year brutal counter-insurgency that included mass killing of Hutu civilians. Although this second, protracted wave of killing fits the typical pattern of a suicidal rebellion, the case as a whole cannot be coded as the victim group provoking its own demise. (This coding could change if evidence were found that the assassination itself was provoked by impending Hutu plans for violence.)

10. Despite its title, the book devotes considerable attention to the strategic nature of genocide.

11. Valentino (2000) makes a similar point about the potential misperceptions of state leaders: "A strategic approach to mass killing does not imply that leaders accurately assess the threats they face. Nor does it suggest that mass killing will always help leaders achieve their goals or solve their problems ... Nevertheless, leaders ultimately act on the basis of their perceptions and beliefs."

12. For example, in 1995 the Minorities at Risk database identified 268 "ethnic or communal groups" worldwide that were "disadvantaged by comparison with other groups in their society", of which only 22 (8%) were engaged in violent rebellion at or above the level of intermediate-scale guerrilla activity. See Gurr (2000). Valentino (2000) notes that "Recent quantitative research on ethnic conflict and genocide has found little correlation between the severity of ethnic, social, economic, and cultural differences and the likelihood of large-scale violence between groups". See also Fearon and Laitin (2003); Hoeffler and Collier (2004).

13. A good primer is Davies (1971b). Perhaps most prolific is Ted Robert Gurr (1970; 1993), who has published numerous versions of his theory.

14. Both quoted in Davies (1971a), which notes that the original theory of Marx and Engels posited revolution as the response of industrial workers to their progressive absolute deprivation under capitalism. However, Marx later wrote that revolution was still inevitable in the face of rising living standards of the proletariat, because "although the enjoyments of the workers have risen, the social satisfaction that they give has fallen in comparison with the increased enjoyments of the capitalist". Thus, according to Marx, relative deprivation of material goods leads to absolute deprivation of social satisfaction, and thence to revolution.

15. His work draws on 'frustration-aggression' theory.

16. A recent version of this theory is found in Goodwin (2001). See also the more general argument in Hirschman (1970).

17. Similarly, Thornton (1964) writes that "terroristic acts often are committed with the express purpose of provoking reprisals". Pye (1964) writes that "The initial decisions of a government confronted with the threat of internal war are usually the most fateful and long-lasting".

18. As early as 1968 a study for the US military found that rebellions tend to occur in rural societies with rough terrain favourable to guerrilla warfare. D.M. Condit, cited in Orlansky (1970). A similar finding was recently made by Fearon and Laitin (1999). Other researchers have discovered that areas of ethnic geographic concentration—that is, when a group is a majority in a local region but a minority in the state as a whole—also favour rebellion, presumably by facilitating mobilization but also possibly by exacerbating the security dilemma with other groups in the state. On this point, Gurr (2000) cites the work of Erik Melander, Monica Duffy Toft, Barry Posen and Stephen Van Evera.

19. See Gurr (2000) on "feedback effects" and the "dynamics of protracted conflict". Unfortunately, a linear causal diagram (p. 70) masks the endogeneity of his theory. A diagram in his previous book (Gurr, 1993, p. 125), containing feedback loops, was more confusing but more explicit about this endogeneity.

20. The main variables, and their underlying variables, are also summarized in the diagram in Gurr (2000, p. 70). *Salience of identity* is a function of: 1) the extent of cultural differentials; 2) relative deprivation; and 3) intensity of past and present conflicts with the state and other groups. *Incentives* for collective action (based on various types of relative deprivation) include: 4) overcoming collective disadvantage; 5) regaining political autonomy; and 6) resisting repression. *Group capacity* for action (i.e. mobilization) is a function of all the preceding variables and 7) territorial concentration (including terrain features); 8) pre-existing group cohesion; 9) intra-group coalition building; and 10) legitimacy of group leaders. *Political opportunities* for action are opened by: 11) state creation or destruction; 12) regime transition including democratization; and 13) leadership transition. *International factors* that can affect all of the above variables include: 14) global norms of group rights; 15) diasporas; 16) diffusion and contagion of ideas and resources between similarly situated but ethnically distinct groups in different states; and 17) other external political and material support. *Domestic political factors* that determine whether ethnopolitical action will be peaceful or militant include: 18) institutions of democracy or authoritarianism; 19) extent of state

resources to accommodate group demands; and 20) state traditions of accommodating or repressing group demands.

21. This theory, from the field of psychology, posits that the frustration from unfulfilled aspirations or expectations is the root cause of aggression. The theory originates with Freud and was formalized and tested originally by Dollar *et al.* (1939). Subsequent studies include Feierabend and Feierabend (1966) and Tanter and Midlarsky (1967). In addition, Gurr (1971) explicitly roots itself in this theory.

22. Some versions of this theory assume rational action but by multiple actors in a non-unitary state to maximize their own utility rather than that of the state. Allison and Halperin (1972).

23. These case studies are drawn from, and fully documented in, Kuperman (2002).

24. As noted by Lebow and Stein (1989), "the reconstructions of participants after the fact ... [are] subject to well-known biases". Accordingly, Lebow and Stein "look for convergent evidence from several participants from each side, and for historical documentation as well".

25. The journalist quoted is Veton Surroi.

26. A similar phenomenon may explain a few earlier suicidal rebellions, for example those in the 19th century by Christian groups in the Balkans against Ottoman authorities, aimed at provoking retaliation that would attract intervention from Christian Europe.

27. A recent report on this phenomenon is discussed in Blustein (2004).

28. On requirements, see Quinlivan (1995). On resources, see O'Hanlon (2003).

29. For suggestions on how to expand global capacity for timely and effective humanitarian military intervention, see Kuperman (2001; 2004a); White House (2004); O'Hanlon (2003).

30. Advocates of this norm do not appear to draw a meaningful distinction between provoked and unprovoked state violence. Interestingly, the 'responsibility to protect' was based on the two cases in my study—Bosnia and Kosovo—plus Rwanda and Somalia. See also Chopra and Weiss (1992); Deng (1995); and Deng *et al.* (1996).

31. In his contribution to this volume Crawford (2006) apportions responsibility for genocidal retaliation between the rebels who provoke it and the international intervenors who create moral hazard that encourages rebellion. He argues that more responsibility adheres to the rebels if moral hazard has been created by a long-standing international norm of intervention rather than an *ad hoc* proximal threat of intervention, because the rebels can anticipate the domestic and international reactions to their rebellion.

References

Allison, G. T. & Halperin, M. H. (1972) Bureaucratic politics: a paradigm and some policy implications, *World Politics*, 24 (Supplement: Theory and Policy in International Relations), pp. 40–79.

Aristotle (1971) Politics, in: J. C. Davies (Ed.), *When Men Revolt and Why* (New York: Free Press).

Baker, T. (1996) On the genealogy of moral hazard, *Texas Law Review*, 75(2), pp. 237–292.

Blustein, P. (2004) IMF says its policies crippled Argentina; internal audit finds warnings were ignored, *Washington Post*, 30 July, p. E1.

Brown, J. (1998) Rebel rebound clouds a deal, *Christian Science Monitor*, 22 October.

Burg, S. L. & Shoup, P.S. (1999) *The War in Bosnia-Herzegovina* (New York: M.E. Sharpe).

Chopra, J. & Weiss, T. G. (1992) Sovereignty is no longer sacrosanct: codifying humanitarian intervention, *Ethics and International Affairs*, 6(1), pp. 95–117.

Clinton, W. J. (1999) Interview, Late Edition, CNN, 20 June, available online at: http://www.cnn.com/ALLPOLITICS/stories/1999/06/20/clinton.transcript/.

Cornwell, R. (1999) "This repellent war crime": a nation helpless as Serbs goad impotent West, *Independent*, 19 January.

Crawford, T. W. (2003) *Pivotal Deterrence: Third Party Statecraft and the Pursuit of Peace* (Ithaca, NY: Cornell University Press).

Crawford, T. W. (2006) Moral hazard, intervention and internal war: a conceptual analysis, in: T.W. Crawford and A.J. Kuperman (Eds.) *Gambling on Humanitarian Intervention*, (London: Routledge).

Davies, J. C. (1971a) Toward a theory of revolution, in: J. C. Davies (Ed.), *When Men Revolt and Why* (New York: Free Press).

Davies, J. C. (1971b) *When Men Revolt and Why* (New York: Free Press).

Dealey, S. (2004) Misreading the truth in Sudan, *New York Times*, 8 August.

Deng, F. (1995) Reconciling sovereignty with responsibility: a basis for international humanitarian action, in: J. Harbeson (Ed.), *Africa in World Politics—Post Cold War Challenges* (Boulder, CO: Westview Press).

Deng, F., Zartman, I. W. & Rothchild, D. (1996) *Sovereignty as Responsibility: Conflict Management in Africa* (Washington, DC: Brookings Institution).

Dollar, J. A., Doob, L., Miller, N., Mowrer, O. & Sears, R. (1939) *Frustration and Aggression* (New Haven, CT: Yale University Press).

Fearon, J. D. & Laitin, D. D. (1999) Weak states, rough terrain, and large-scale ethnic violence since 1945, paper presented at the annual meeting of the American Political Science Association, Atlanta, GA, 2–5 September.

Fearon, J. D. & Laitin, D. D. (2003) Ethnicity, insurgency, and civil war, *American Political Science Review*, 97(1), pp. 75–90.

Feierabend, I. K. & Feierabend, R.L. (1966) Aggressive behaviors within polities, 1948–1962: a cross-national study, *Journal of Conflict Resolution*, 10, pp. 249–271.

Fein, H. (1979) *Accounting for Genocide* (Chicago: University of Chicago Press).

Fein, H. (1990) Genocide: a sociological perspective, *Current Sociology*, 38(1) pp. 1–126.

Fein, H. (1993) Accounting for genocide after 1945: theories and some findings, *International Journal on Group Rights*, 1, pp. 79–106.

Fein, H. (1994) Patrons, prevention and punishment of genocide: observations on Bosnia and Rwanda, in: H. Fein (Ed.), *The Prevention of Genocide: Rwanda and Yugoslavia Reconsidered* (New York: Institute for the Study of Genocide).

George, A. L. (1979) Case studies and theory development: the method of structured, focused comparison, in: P. G. Lauren (Ed.), *Diplomacy: New Approaches in History, Theory and Policy* (New York: Free Press).

Goodwin, J. (2001) *No Other Way Out: States and Revolutionary Movements, 1945–1991* (New York: Cambridge University Press).

Gow, J. (1997) *Triumph of the Lack of Will* (New York: Columbia University Press).

Gude, E. W. (1971) Political violence in Venezuela: 1958–1964, in: J. C. Davies (Ed.), *When Men Revolt and Why* (New York: Free Press).

Gurr, T. R. (1970) *Why Men Rebel* (Princeton, NJ: Center of International Studies).

Gurr, T. R. (1971) A causal model of civil strife, in: J. C. Davies (Ed.), *When Men Revolt and Why* (New York: Free Press).

Gurr, T. R. (1993) *Minorities at Risk* (Washington, DC: US Institute of Peace).

Gurr, T. R. (2000) *Peoples Versus States* (Washington, DC: US Institute of Peace).

Harff, B. (1987) The etiology of genocides, in: I. Wallimann & M. N. Dobkowski (Eds), *Genocide and the Modern Age: Etiology and Case Studies of Mass Death* (New York: Greenwood Press).

Harff, B. (1994) A theoretical model of genocides and politicides, *Journal of Ethno-Development*, 4(1), pp. 25–30.

Harff, B. (2003) No lessons learned from the Holocaust? Assessing risks of genocide and political mass murder since 1955, *American Political Science Review*, 97(1), pp. 57–73.

Harff, B. & Gurr, T. R. (1988) Toward an empirical theory of genocides and politicides, *International Studies Quarterly*, 32, pp. 359–371.

Harff, B. & Gurr, TR (1989) Victims of the state: genocides, politicides, and group repression since 1945, *International Review of Victimology*, 1, pp. 1–19.

Hirschman, A. O. (1970) *Exit, Voice, and Loyalty* (Cambridge, MA: Harvard University Press).

Hoeffler, A. & Collier, P. (2004) Greed and grievance in civil wars, *Oxford Economic Papers*, available online at: http://users.ox.ac.uk/~ball0144/research.htm

International Commission on Intervention and State Sovereignty (2001) *The Responsibility to Protect*, December, available online at: http://www.iciss.gc.ca/Report-English.asp.

Johnstone, D. (1998) Notes on the Kosovo problem and the international community, *Dialogue*, 25, available online at: http://www.bglink.com/business/dialogue/diana.html

Kornhauser, W. (1964) Rebellion and political development, in: H. Eckstein (Ed.), *Internal War: Problems and Approaches* (New York: Free Press).

Krain, M. (1997) State-sponsored mass murder: the onset and severity of genocides and politicides, *Journal of Conflict Resolution*, 41(3), pp. 331–360.

Kuperman, A. J. (1996) The other lesson of Rwanda: mediators sometimes do more damage than good, *SAIS Review*, 16(1), pp. 221–240.

Kuperman, A. J. (1999) Once again, peacekeepers arrive too late, *Wall Street Journal*, 21 September.

Kuperman, A. J. (2001) *The Limits of Humanitarian Intervention: Genocide in Rwanda* (Washington, DC: Brookings Institution).

Kuperman, A. J. (2002) Tragic challenges and the moral hazard of humanitarian intervention: how and why ethnic groups provoke genocidal retaliation, unpublished doctoral dissertation, MIT.

Kuperman, A. J. (2004a) Humanitarian hazard: revisiting doctrines of intervention, *Harvard International Review*, 26(1), pp. 64–68.

Kuperman, A. J. (2004b) Next steps in Sudan, *Washington Post*, 28 September, p. A27.

Kuperman, A. J. (2004c) Provoking genocide: a revised history of the Rwandan Patriotic Front, *Journal of Genocide Research*, 6(1), pp. 61–84.

Lebow, R. N. & Stein, J. G. (1989) Rational deterrence theory: I think, therefore I deter, *World Politics*, 41(2), pp. 208–224.

Little, A. (2000a) How NATO was sucked into Kosovo conflict, *Sunday Telegraph*, 27 February, p. 29.

Little, A. (2000b) Moral combat: NATO at war, BBC2, 12 March, available online at: http://news.bbc.co.uk/hi/english/static/events/panorama/transcripts/transcript_12_03_00.txt.

Loza, T. (1998) Kosovo Albanians closing the ranks, *Transitions*, 5(5), p. 27.

Matthews, M. (1998) NATO struggles to contain fighting peacefully in Balkans, *Baltimore Sun*, 5 July.

Matthews, M. & Bowman, T. (1999) In Kosovo talks, time running out, *Baltimore Sun*, 20 February.

McAdam, D. (1982) *Political Process and the Development of Black Insurgency, 1930–1970* (Chicago: University of Chicago Press).

Nyman, J. A. (2001) The theory of the demand for health insurance, University of Minnesota, 4 January, available online at: http://www.econ.umn.edu/workingpapers/nyman.pdf.

O'Hanlon, M. E. (2003) *Expanding Global Military Capacity for Humanitarian Intervention* (Washington, DC: Brookings Institution).

Orlansky, J. (1970) *The State of Research on Internal War* (Arlington, VA: Institute for Defense Analyses).

du Preez, P. (1994) *The Psychology of Mass Murder* (London: Boyars/Bowerdean).

Pye, L.W. (1964) The roots of insurgency, in: H. Eckstein (Ed.), *Internal War: Problems and Approaches* (New York: Free Press).

Quinlivan, J. T. (1995) Force requirements in stability operations, *Parameters*, 25(4), pp. 59–69.

Rose, M. (1998) *Fighting for Peace: Bosnia 1994* (London: Harvill Press).

Rummel, R. J. (1992) *Democide: Nazi Genocide and Mass Murder* (New Brunswick, NJ: Transaction Publishers).

Samyn, E. (1998) NATO seeks Russian cooperation for end to conflict, *Daily Yomiuri*, 10 July.

Schelling, T. C. (1966) *Arms and Influence* (New Haven, CT: Yale University Press).

Schwartz, D. C. (1971) A theory of revolutionary behavior, in: J.C. Davies (Ed.), *When Men Revolt and Why* (New York: Free Press).

Shue, H. (2004) Limiting sovereignty, in: J. M. Welsh (Ed.), *Humanitarian Intervention and International Relations*, pp. 11–28 (Oxford: Oxford University Press).

Smith, R. (1987) Human destructiveness and politics: the twentieth century as an Age of Genocide, in: I. Wallimann & M. N. Dobkowski (Eds), *Genocide and the Modern Age: Etiology and Case Studies of Mass Death* (New York: Greenwood Press).

Tanter, R. & Midlarsky, M. (1967) A theory of revolution, *Journal of Conflict Resolution*, 21, pp. 264–280.

Tarrow, S. (1994) *Power in Movement: Social Movements, Collective Action, and Politics* (New York: Cambridge University Press).

Thornton, T. P. (1964) Terror as a weapon, in: H. Eckstein (Ed.), *Internal War: Problems and Approaches* (New York: Free Press).

Tilly, C. (1978) *From Mobilization to Revolution* (Reading, MA: Addison-Wesley).

United Nations (2004) *A More Secure World: Our Shared Responsibility*, High Level Panel on Threats, Challenges and Change, 1 December, available online at: http://www.un.org/secureworld/.

Valentino, B. (2000) Final solutions: the causes of genocide and mass killing, *Security Studies*, 9(2), pp. 1–62.

Valentino, B. (2004) *Final Solutions: Mass Killing and Genocide in the 20th Century* (Ithaca, NY: Cornell University Press).

Van Evera, S. (1997) *Guide to Methods for Students of Political Science* (Ithaca, NY: Cornell University Press).

Wheeler, N. J. (2004) The humanitarian responsibilities of sovereignty: explaining the development of a new norm of military intervention for humanitarian purposes in international society, in: J. M. Welsh (Ed.), *Humanitarian Intervention and International Relations* (Oxford: Oxford University Press).

White House (2004) G-8 Action Plan: expanding global capability for peace support operations, Office of the Press Secretary, 10 June.

Wintour, P. (1999) Serb godfather at bay; call for talks delays threat of force, *Observer*, 24 January.

Moral Hazard, Intervention and Internal War: A Conceptual Analysis

TIMOTHY W. CRAWFORD

Although intervention is typically thought of as a remedy for internal wars, it may cause as well as calm them (Kuperman, 2004; 2003a, b; 1996; Crawford, 2004; 2003; 2001; 1998; Rowlands & Carment, 1998; Pham, 2004; Lischer, 2003; Rauchhaus, 2000; Bloom, 1999). The concept of moral hazard suggests one way in which it might do so.[1] In barest form the idea is that the prospect of outside support tempts groups, which would otherwise be cautious and peaceful, to run risks and use violence in challenging their governments. Although the underlying problem is not new to international politics (see, for example, Snyder, 1984), and the concept is not new to students and practitioners of insurance, law and economics (Baker, 1996), applying it to intervention is. If this conceptual crossover is fruitful, it will call attention to aspects of intervention "which are of theoretical importance but often not readily apparent" in other approaches to the subject (Oppenheim, 1975, pp. 303–304). The purpose here is to elucidate the basis for the conceptual crossover, and some principles for appraising it.

One reason moral hazard is not 'apparent' in most work on intervention, no doubt, is that many students (and advocates) of intervention bridle at the normative costs of viewing the subject from that standpoint. For this reason a frank account of those liabilities is desirable.[2] But before we can do such accounting, we need first to clarify the concept's internal logic, and its descriptive implications and limitations. We will do so in three steps. First, we will explore the links to our concept of moral hazard from kindred but more general concepts of social science. This will reveal the lineage of important aspects of its meaning and amplify its heuristic power. Second, we will hone in on the essential propositions which explain how intervention may cause internal wars, and indicate empirical patterns which must exist if such explanations are to be descriptively valid. Third, we will set out four main types of explanation implied by the concept, and discuss issues raised by each.

Kindred Concepts: Perverse Incentives and Negative Precedents

Moral hazard is an effect of insurance. But insurance, as Baker (1996) notes, "is not simply something provided by 'insurance companies'". In the larger sense it "is provided any time that one party's actions have consequences for the risk of loss borne by another" (p. 272). Whether domestic or international, political actions and relationships often involve shifting and sharing risk in ways that influence actors' incentives. Thus the problem of moral hazard in intervention is not unusual but rather part of the familiar fabric of political life. We will begin, then, by discussing two terms much employed in the study of politics—perverse incentives and negative precedents—which inform the particular concept of moral hazard advanced here.

An incentive, according to the *Oxford English Dictionary* (1989) is something that "incites to action"—a stimulus to behaviour. Perverse incentives stimulate undesirable behaviour by promising to reward it. They were, for example, at the centre of controversy over the 'poor-law' reforms in Britain in the 1830s. "The leading economists of the time", wrote Jacob Viner, "all emphasized the allegedly injurious effects on the productive capacity and the will to work and to save of the poor which would result from generous, long sustained, and assured poor-relief to the able-bodied...the humanitarians and the clergy stressed in opposition the moral and political rights of the needy to be given food and shelter with a minimum of humiliation" (1940, pp. 3–4).[3] A different problem of perverse incentives was raised by Arnold Wolfers in 1945, when he warned against adding to the United Nations Charter a provision for "revision of treaties and of prior international decisions". The problem, he argued, was that "any explicit promise of future revision of territorial settlements...would carry with it serious dangers to the peace. [Such] encouragement of territorial revisionism is an incentive to aggressive war preparations"(1945, p. 10). In another, very different context, US nuclear strategists determined that by deploying vulnerable deterrent forces—which could only be used in a surprise attack—you would give your enemy an "incentive to strike first" (Jervis, 1989, ch. 5). Doing so, Albert Wohlstetter (1959) famously observed, "would tend to provoke rather than deter general war".

A precedent, according to the *Oxford English Dictionary* (1989) is "an example that is followed or copied"—a guide to behaviour. A negative precedent guides behaviour in an undesirable direction. Closely related to Wolfers's concern is the quintessential negative precedent problem in international security—'appeasement'. As Quincy Wright explained:

> Such a policy [of appeasement] tends to stimulate aggression by others. Instead of deterring, it encourages potential aggressors. Successful crime tends to spread. The League's weakness in the face of Japan's aggression in Manchuria in 1931 encouraged Mussolini to aggress against Ethiopia in 1935. This in turn encouraged Hitler to violate Locarno in 1936. The success of this episode precipitated further aggression by the Axis powers in Spain, China, Austria, Czechoslovakia, Lithuania, Albania, Danzig, and Poland in the following years. (Wright, 1965, p. 1327)

Another hardy perennial of international security is the negative precedent created by using partition to resolve internal wars: the issue being whether "partition in a few countries. . .encourage[s] partition elsewhere" (Sambanis, 2000, p. 440). E. H. Carr passed this verdict on the negative precedent problem of using partition to achieve 'self-determination' of minorities:

> Far from providing, as Woodrow Wilson and others believed in 1919, the infallible short cut to a political paradise—[it] has incurred discredit as the apparent cause of some of our most intractable political and economic problems. . .[it] fostered the disintegration of existing political units, and favored the creation of a multiplicity of smaller units. . .at a time when the survival of small independent states has been rendered problematical. (Carr, 1942, pp. 40, 51, 52)[4]

One final current illustration of negative precedent deserves mention. Many critics of the Bush Doctrine and its apparent application in the Iraq war charged that it set a dangerous and negative precedent which will lead other countries to launch pre-emptive wars, some of which will harm US interests (e.g. Record, 2003; Heisbourg, 2003; Dombrowski & Payne, 2003). "A more dangerous, illegitimate norm and example can hardly be imagined", writes Paul Schroeder. "It completely subverts previous standards for judging the legitimacy of resorts to war, justifying any number of wars hitherto considered unjust and aggressive. It would, in fact, justify almost any attack by any state on any other for almost any reason" (Schroeder, 2002).

The logics of perverse incentive and negative precedent which inform our concept of moral hazard are, then, familiar mechanisms of war causation. It is useful to distinguish between the two ideas because, while negative precedents always pose perverse incentives, perverse incentives do not only arise from negative precedents. Perverse incentives may also be caused by novel and untested—in other words, *un*precedented—policies and actions, although resonant negative precedents would tend to exacerbate them. So the concept of perverse incentives subsumes the concept of negative precedent, and when it comes to the logic of moral hazard, perverse incentives are the more fundamental of the two.

Arguments about the moral hazard of intervention often juggle the two ideas, but they do not have to go together in a given use of the concept. For example, one may argue that a specific form of intervention, at a particular juncture in a conflict, introduced perverse incentives which caused it to escalate in an unintended way. Thus I have argued elsewhere that, in the autumn of 1998, NATO inadvertently caused the Kosovo conflict to escalate by imposing a ceasefire on Serbia, while failing to apply matching pressure on the KLA. This allowed the KLA to "reconstitute quickly as a political and fighting force" and take the offensive (Crawford, 2001, pp. 513–514). In this "situation-contingent" form, the moral hazard is the result of perverse incentives which do not derive their causal force from negative precedents. By contrast, one can shift to a higher point of view, and emphasize the moral hazard problem arising from the negative precedents set by repeated interventions. Thus one postulate in Kuperman's theory of the moral hazard of humanitarian intervention is that, "Each time the West intervenes militarily on behalf of a subordinate group, it increases expectations of future such interventions...and thereby encourages further uprisings" (Kuperman, 2003a, p. 75; see also Kuperman, 2004, p. 67).

How the two strands of meaning in these terms carry over to the concept of moral hazard should now be obvious. The first strand comes from the nouns (incentive, precedent), which denote some influence upon the behaviour of actors. The second strand comes from the adjectives (perverse, negative) which indicate that the resulting behaviour is undesirable. That it is undesirable suggests that it is not anticipated, although, as we shall see, this need not always be the case. In the discussion which follows, we will delve deeper into this question of unintended consequences and the role it plays in the moral hazard concept.

Specifications

Now we must delineate the essential elements of our concept of moral hazard. The *Oxford English Dictionary* defines moral hazard as "the lack of incentive to avoid risk where there is protection against its consequences". If we substitute antonyms for the terms 'lack' and 'avoid' we come close to the causal-core of the concept—the presence of incentives to take risk where there is protection (or the expectation of protection) against its consequences.

Where do these incentives come from? Not from thin air, but sooner or later, from the actions of others. Moral hazard is not immaculately conceived: it is fathered by earthly potentates. Moral hazard is thus a 'relational' concept which denotes "a relationship of interaction"—more or less direct—between actors (Oppenheim, 1975, p. 287). That relationship involves *influence*, exercised by those who create moral hazard incentives, over the behaviour of those who respond to them. In this way, the concept of moral hazard forwards a potentially valid causal explanation of the behaviour of political actors exposed to such perverse incentives.

Thus, for Dane Rowlands and David Carment, the moral hazard of intervention occurs when "the intervener's own actions cause the combatants to prefer conflict escalation to moderation". The intervenor's actions create "incentive structures" which lead the antagonists "to reduce their effort to avoid calamity" (1998, p. 271). Similarly, Robert Rauchhaus has argued that something akin to moral hazard occurs "when a third party, through actions or promises to act, creates an incentive structure that encourages others to take risks or actions that they otherwise would avoid" (Rauchhaus, 2003).[5] Thus the impetus for the rebels' action derives from incentives in their *strategic context* (created by an intervenor) rather than from changes in the substance of their goals. That is, intervention or the prospect of it does not transform a contented minority into malcontents, but rather, changes the environment in which, and the means by which, malcontents pursue political change. Moral hazard emboldens malcontents, it does not create them.[6]

But that proposition leaves out two important things that we often mean to evoke when we apply the concept to intervention in internal war. The first is that the outcome is perverse. Here we must ask—perverse for whom? The answer is the intervenor. Hence there must be a basic conflict between the intervenor's goals and interests (as it perceives them) and the risky behaviour resulting from the incentives it creates.[7] The second, which adds an ironic twist, has to do with the intervenor's intentions rather than interests. The intervenor, it is argued, did not intend to cause the perverse consequences. As Kuperman puts it "moral hazard is when efforts to ensure against risk *inadvertently* promote risk-taking behavior" (Kuperman, 2003b, p. 142). There is an important distinction between unintended and inadvertent consequences, which we will tease out below. Here, however, it is sufficient to emphasize the meaning they share in common: that the intervenor did not create the incentive in order to induce the perverse outcome. In sum, our concept of moral hazard comprises three descriptive propositions:

1. The rebels' resort to political violence stems from incentives created by the intervenor's actions, and *not* by change in their underlying motivation. (We will call this the *incentive effect.*)
2. That result is harmful to the intervenor's goals and interests. (We will call this the *perverse condition.*)
3. To induce that result was *not* the intervenor's intention. (We will call this the *un-intention condition.*)

Paying close attention to these three elements of the concept helps to clear away cases which do not involve, or only seem to involve, moral hazard. When an outsider intentionally foments internal war in another country in order to topple the government, you do not have moral hazard but instead subversion. Likewise, it is inapt to say that moral hazard operated if the intervenor did not consciously seek to trigger rebellion but doing so was consistent with its interests, and may even have advanced them. Some unintended consequences are fortuitous rather than unfortunate or, as Robert Merton put it, "undesired effects are not always undesirable effects" (Merton, 1936, p. 895; see also Elster, 1989, pp. 96–97). In the early 1970s India's purpose in sheltering East Pakistan's beleaguered Bengali refugees (many of whom were guerrilla fighters), and its forceful intervention which followed, may not have been to facilitate Pakistan's disintegration (Blechman & Kaplan, 1978, p. 177).[8] But, given India's enmity with Pakistan, and its obvious interest in hegemony on the subcontinent, the independence of Bangladesh can hardly be called a perverse consequence of Indian humanitarian policy.

However, the combination of the three propositions does not always yield clear lines of demarcation. Indeed, ambiguity may arise in relation to the third proposition—the un-intention condition. The ambiguity turns on whether the perverse consequences were "unintended but not unanticipated" by the intervenor (Jervis, 1997, p. 61, n. 99). Here it really is "the thought that counts".[9] A problem of indirect effect thus arises when an intervenor knowingly acts in a way that creates an incentive to rebellion, but doing so is not its primary political goal. If the anticipated but unintended side-effect is also harmful to the intervenor's interests (i.e. perverse), then the moral hazard concept certainly applies.[10] But this looser form of the un-intention condition—which includes anticipated perverse side-effects—furnishes an explanation for a less puzzling sort of political phenomenon. Although a doctor may not primarily aim to kill a foetus we do not find it strange if she chooses to do so in order to save a mother's life (Baert, 1991, p. 205). Similarly, it is edifying but not startling to learn that stoking a civil war was part of the price an intervenor was willing to pay to accomplish another political goal, such as providing aid to starving civilians.

This is very different from a policy that *unwittingly* leads to unwanted results.[11] The distinction points to a tighter form of the un-intention condition, which holds that moral hazard occurs *only* when the perverse consequences are not anticipated by the intervenor. Although the primary causal relationship in Kuperman's theory of the moral hazard of humanitarian intervention is the link between the perverse incentives posed by intervenors and the violent challenges of rebels, one may extrapolate such a larger moral hazard theory from his treatment of indirect effects—which sometimes include a genocidal backlash by the challenged government.[12] In this more capacious version, the dependent variable of the moral hazard of humanitarian intervention would be the second-order and unanticipated effect of the intervenor's efforts—the triggering of genocidal wrath against groups emboldened to rebel by the prospect of intervention.

Given the spread of meaning between looser and tighter forms, a number of points are worth noting. First, while the tighter form is likely to capture the most startling cases, there will be few of them. Decision makers are rarely so blind to the probable negative effects of their action. The looser form will cover a broader range of cases, but these are likely to be less puzzling. Second, the consequences captured by the looser form are more likely to be the direct result of perverse incentives: their causal proximity makes them easier to anticipate. Conversely, the consequences covered in the tighter form are likely to be the indirect 'second-order' results of perverse incentives: this layer of causal distance makes them harder to anticipate. Thus, to return to the argument above, the perversion lies in the gulf between the intervenor's intention to help an oppressed group, and the indirect result of those efforts: a genocidal government crackdown on the minority. The truly awful consequence comes *after* the direct effect of the intervenor's action—an energized rebellion. And it is this second order, less predictable, choice made by the retaliating government which helps to explain why the intervenor did not anticipate the perverse results.

This raises another critical issue, namely, whether the moral hazard concept is appropriate if only the second-order effect is perverse and unanticipated. To put this concretely: US policy makers in 1998 did not pursue a policy of humanitarian intervention towards Kosovo in order to cause Belgrade to massacre and uproot ethnic Albanians by the thousands. But they did anticipate that an emboldened KLA would weaken Serb rule in Kosovo and, moreover, undermine Milosevic's grip on Serbian politics. Indeed, some argue that they wanted to do precisely those things (Jatras, 2000), as well as save Kosovo Albanian lives. If that were true, the unanticipated and unwanted results only occurred after the intervenor had taken action that it knew and hoped would encourage the rebels. But does the concept of moral hazard still fit if inducing rebellion was an expected and desired side-effect of intervention, and it was only the government's sledgehammer response which spoiled things?

I would argue that it does still hold, in an attenuated sense, because the initial catalyst for the perverse results remains an incentive to take risk, in the form of protection against losses, provided by the intervenor. With that core condition still central to the causal story—which leads to perverse and unanticipated results—the basic elements of an explanation based on moral hazard are present. But it is safe to say that the question is open to debate, and that critics will view this point, among others made here, as 'stretching' the moral hazard concept too far (e.g. Grigorian, 2006; Rauchhaus, 2006).

Meanwhile, it will be useful for scholars to distinguish between 'thick' and 'thin' versions of moral hazard. Thinner versions, which will occur more frequently, will arise when intervenors indirectly induce perverse and unanticipated behaviour; or when intervenors directly induce perverse but anticipated behaviour. Thick moral hazard occurs when the intervenor directly induces perverse behaviour it did not anticipate. These differences in meaning will be explored below, where we will discuss more concretely how the concept can be used to explain outcomes.

Four Explanatory Contexts

The concept developed above describes an influence relationship which may explain why some internal wars occur. The next task is to map out the main contours of such explanations and better understand their strengths and weaknesses. In order to focus on the key driver of these explanations—i.e. the incentive effect—we will refer to a variety of cases of 'non-humanitarian' intervention in internal war. We will do so because these cases display the incentive effect but are not clouded by the problems of un-intention and perverse consequences. Once we have clarified these patterns of explanation, we will consider implications for those latter two elements of the concept.

Remote versus Proximate Causes of Internal War

Let us begin with the difference between 'remote' or 'underlying' causes of war and 'immediate' or 'proximate' causes of war (Bernard, 1972, p. 238). The former are "long term causes" of tension and conflict, while the latter are those "that actually trigger war" (Lebow, 1981, p.1). To see how the distinction can be applied to internal wars, consider the Spanish Civil War. Historian Raymond Sontag's diagnosis highlights its underlying internal causes and dismisses the importance of outside influence:

> [It] was an affair of the Spanish people, and not of outsiders, whether the USSR or Nazi Germany or Fascist Italy. All three swung into action once the civil war began and greatly influenced the course and the outcome of the civil war; but the civil war was the outcome of hatreds which, over the course of more than a century, had been building up ever more explosively among the people of once proud and powerful but now weak and impoverished Spain. (Sontag, 1971, p. 300)

But, given the role Spain's civil war played in the breakdown of peace in Europe, certainly the timing of its outbreak matters, and when it comes to explaining that, and understanding whether the conflict could have been averted in the critical short term, a focus on underlying causes offers little traction. To understand why the Spanish right revolted in 1936, the social and political turmoil of the 1930s that accompanied the rise of the Spanish left is obviously important—but so is the parallel rise of fascism in Italy and, most of all, Italy's direct efforts to fuel a Nationalist revolt. Sontag's view would have us dismiss as unimportant the fact that in 1932 and 1934 Mussolini financed right-wing plots against the Spanish republic, and that coup plotters on the Spanish right were expecting even greater support in 1936 (Salerno, 2002, pp. 16–17). Their expectations in this regard were richly fulfilled.[13] Of course, for Mussolini, the consequences were neither perverse nor unintended. But the point is not that this is an instance of internal war caused by moral hazard, rather that it is an instance of internal war at least partly caused by a proximate incentive to the rebel group, provided by an outsider poised to underwrite the risks of rebellion.[14]

Now consider the prospect of intervention as a remote—rather than proximate—cause of internal war. To illustrate this view, we may look back to the American Revolution. Contrary to the flattering idea that the rebellion was an act of separation from European entanglements, the Founding Fathers were in fact emboldened to challenge British rule by the obvious willingness of France to succour the rebellion—indeed, it was an explicit element of French policy from 1764 onward, and implicit for long before that (see DeConde, 1978, pp. 23--25). While the many particulars of the deteriorating relationship between Great Britain and the American colonies in the early 1770s undoubtedly mattered, the long-standing lure of French support coloured the Founders' judgements about the potentialities of open insurrection.

A similar argument can be made that Confederate decisions to secede from—and wage war upon--the Union in 1861 were informed by long and widely held beliefs about "the coercive economic power of cotton, on which English and French textile industries were dependent", which encouraged Southerners to calculate that, in the event of war, those countries would be forced "to recognize the Confederacy as independent and to end any long war by intervening on their side" (DeConde, 1978, p. 227). Again, to look at the origins of the US civil war in this way is not to dismiss the fundamental importance of the central issue at stake—slavery—or the more proximate factors affecting political decisions taken on both sides of the Mason-Dixon Line. But it is to suggest that the way the central issue was resolved could have been different had the secessionist leaders had a different background assumption about the international political situation, i.e. that the European powers would isolate rather than intervene in an American civil war. That background assumption, therefore, may be seen as a remote cause of the war.

Proximate causes of war are, as a general rule, more subject to political manipulation and human choice than remote causes, which tend to be embedded in the history and structure of a political context (Brodie, 1973, p. 316; Waltz, 1959, pp. 232–233; Wright, 1935). This is even more likely to be true when the proximate cause is an incentive (intended or not) resulting from a conscious policy choice. If it were not, the very idea of statecraft would be dubious. Thus, a 'thin' conception is likely to more accurately describe the reality of a case in which moral hazard is a proximate cause of internal war, because it is likely that the perverse consequence was anticipated, even if not intended, by the intervenor.

One implication, then, is that the creators of proximate moral hazard must bear greater causal, and thus moral, responsibility for the resulting violence, for two reasons. First, because, given the close link between the incentive and the unwanted behaviour, the intervenors should have been better able to foresee the direct consequences of their policy. The premise here is not that decision makers never misjudge the direct consequences of policy choices, but rather that they are more likely to judge correctly and anticipate direct consequences than indirect ones. Second, they bear greater causal and thus moral responsibility because, given the close proximity between their actions and the consequences, decision makers should have greater ability to alter the trajectory of violence, at least in the short term, by adjusting the policy which creates the perverse incentives.[15]

By the same token, when moral hazard is a remote cause, a greater weight of moral responsibility shifts to those who choose to exploit the prospect of protection for political gain, again for two reasons. First, these actors are in a better position to foresee the direct consequences of their decision to act upon the moral hazard incentive. Second, these actors will have greater ability to adjust their behaviour in ways that modify those consequences once they begin to hit home. In short, the unintended and unanticipated negative consequences (state retaliation) of a remote moral hazard (prospect of humanitarian intervention) are likely to be intended and anticipated, even if not desired, by the actors (rebels) who seek to reap the potential benefits of the perverse incentive. For that reason, they must take more blame for the consequences.

Singular versus Plural Domain of Influence

The concept of moral hazard may denote a *singular* influence relationship unique to the particulars of a given conflict, or a *plural* pattern of influence which exerts a similar and wide-ranging effect on many such conflicts. The distinction relates to the explanatory domain of a particular use of the concept. In other words, who and how many are the actors subject to the influence relationship? It is important to be explicit about domain when we use the concept of moral hazard, because, as Robert Dahl put it, "any statement about influence that does not include the domain and scope it refers to verges on being meaningless" (Dahl, 1984, p. 27).[16] How is the distinction between a singular and plural domain manifest in empirical applications of the moral hazard concept? Again, it is useful to step back and consider cases which highlight the incentive effect.

Consider the 1960 London–Zurich Accords which inaugurated the Republic of Cyprus after the withdrawal of British rule. A crucial element of the agreements was the 'Treaty of Alliance', which made Britain, Greece and Turkey external guarantors of the Republic's delicately balanced constitution—a power-sharing bargain between the Greek Cypriot majority and the Turkish Cypriot minority. The whole arrangement quickly came undone as factions on both sides took steps certain to undermine stability. One could argue that this risky behaviour was influenced by a specific moral hazard built into the Accords—the commitment of obviously partisan outsiders to police Cypriot compliance. In practice this meant that malcontents on both sides of the ethnic divide could bank on the backing of strong outside supporters as they pushed their agendas to the breaking point (see Crawford, 2003, pp. 105–108). It should be clear, then, that in this explanation the incentive-effect operates in a singular domain: the actors subject to it are, specifically, the radical ethnic factions on Cyprus.

How, in this instance and more generally, does the singular domain shape the way we think about the role of perverse and unintended consequences? First, the creators of moral hazard are more likely to anticipate the unintended consequences. While, in the Cyprus case, this is not true for the British, it is true for Greece and Turkey, who were brought into the pact, not because they were impartial, but because they were *extremely* partial to one side. Both intended to vigorously uphold the political position of their ethnic kin in Cyprus. Britain *hoped* that Athens and Ankara would restrain the local parties but, by the same token, it had to be anticipated—by all concerned—that they might do the reverse. In other words, the perverse consequences were almost certainly anticipated, if not intended, by those who created the incentives. This in turn suggests that the creators of the incentives had the capacity, if not the will, to adjust their policies in ways to counteract the results.

Compare that limited pattern of influence to the one implied in the proposition that "hostile international environments spur internal conflict as outside states back rebel groups in enemy countries" (David, 1997, p. 554). Here a condition in the international system, caused by competing powers who, ultimately, create the incentives, engenders a 'contagion' of internal wars. This is the reasoning behind Thucydides' explanation for the wave of rebellions loosed by the clash of Athens and Sparta:

> the whole Hellenic world was convulsed, struggles being everywhere made by the popular chiefs to bring in the Athenians, and by the oligarchs to introduce the [Spartans] ... With an alliance always at the command of either faction for the hurt of their adversaries and their own corresponding advantage, opportunities for bringing in the foreigner were never wanting to the revolutionary parties ... Revolution thus ran its course from city to city (1982, pp. 198–199; see also Price, 2001).

How does such a plural domain of influence shape the way we think about the role of perverse and unintended consequences? First, it implies a greater degree of separation between the intentions of the creators of the incentives and the perverse results in the aggregate. Because there is that larger layer of complexity and indeterminacy, inadvertence almost certainly plays a larger role in the description of the overall influence relationship. In other words, we have much stronger grounds for inferring that the results—at least in the aggregate—were not anticipated by those who created the incentives.

We can draw these considerations together in a four-fold typology of moral hazard explanations (see Table 1). *Acute* moral hazard acts as a proximate cause in a singular domain. *Chronic* moral hazard acts as a remote cause in a singular domain. *Contagious* moral hazard acts as a proximate cause in a plural domain. And *Pervasive* moral hazard acts as a remote cause in a plural domain. Each type embodies a particular set of issues and implications which need to be recognized and addressed when the moral hazard concept is used in that context. These will be illustrated and discussed below.

Acute moral hazard (proximate cause and singular domain). Acute moral hazard involves situation-contingent perverse incentives—created by potential or actual intervenors—which intrude into a simmering and volatile conflict. The incentives set off an escalation to violence on the part of the rebels. The domain of that incentive's influence is limited to those particular rebels in that particular case. Kuperman provides an apt

Table 1. Types of moral hazard

	Proximate cause	Remote cause
Singular scope	*Acute* Bush's call for Iraqi army coup triggers Kurdish/Shiite uprisings	*Chronic* Long-term US involvement in Liberia perpetuates its instability
Plural scope	*Contagious* NATO's rescue of KLA spurs rebellion in Macedonia and Presevo	*Pervasive* Norm of humanitarian intervention encourages rebellions

illustration of this pattern of explanation in his discussion of the Kurdish and Shiite rebellions in Iraq in the wake of the first Gulf war (2003a, p. 60). Those minorities, he writes, had "long been disgruntled due to discrimination at the hands" of the Sunni ruling elite, led by Saddam Hussein. During the 1980s both groups had rebelled and been harshly suppressed, so that, in the few years immediately preceding the first Gulf war, they were quiescent. But during the US war against Iraq in 1991, Washington undertook measures to encourage Iraqis to, as President George H. W. Bush put it, "take matters into their own hands" and topple Hussein. The intention of the Bush administration, apparently, was not to incite the Kurds and Shiites to rebel, but rather, "to encourage a coup from within the Sunni elite of the Iraqi Army". Nevertheless, just days after "the Gulf War ended", writes Kuperman, "the Kurds and the Shiites did indeed rise up, and Saddam predictably responded by ordering his army to crush the rebellions", while the USA stood idly by.

In this instance, the following elements stand out. First, the incentive-effect arises as a stark and marked shift in the rebels' strategic context, acting as an almost immediate trigger for rebellions long in the making. Second, the domain of that incentive's influence is crisply delimited: only Kurds and Shiites in Iraq are emboldened by it. There is no cascade of similar uprisings by Kurds and Shiites, or other minorities, elsewhere in the region. Third, it does not appear that negative precedents played a role in driving the perverse incentive effect. There was no prior history of the USA intervening successfully to support ethnic rebellions in Iraq.[17] And it was only after the rebellions were crushed that the precedent-setting humanitarian safe-zones were created in Iraq under UN authority, which would raise expectations for such intervention throughout the decade. Fourth, if we take Bush administration officials at their word regarding their intentions in calling for Iraqis to take matters into their own hands, then it would appear to be at least an instance of 'thin' moral hazard. Neither the immediate effect of the incentive (the Kurdish and Shiite uprising), nor the indirect consequences (Saddam's devastating crackdown) were intended or desired by US policy makers.

Whether it was 'thick' moral hazard, however, turns on an important lingering question, namely, whether Bush administration officials *anticipated* that a potential side-effect of inciting a coup by Sunni army officers could be the emboldening of Kurdish and Shiite rebels.[18] Only if they had failed to consider this possibility in their decision making would we have an instance of thick moral hazard.

Chronic moral hazard (remote cause and singular domain).   In this context, the hazardous incentive is a background, long-standing factor which sets the stage for rebellion sparked by a more immediate cause or combination of causes. The incentive's domain is limited to that particular case—it is, in other words, highly context-dependent.

A useful illustration of this pattern may be discerned in the sequence of civil wars that rocked Liberia between the late 1980s and 2003. They started with the rebellions led by Charles Taylor and Prince Johnson, which in 1990 toppled strongman Samuel Doe (whom the USA backed in the 1980s, but abandoned as the Cold War ended). The fighting continued to rage afterwards between Taylor's and Johnson's factions, despite the intervention of a regional African peacekeeping force. When Johnson was eliminated, there was a brief lull, leading to Taylor's election as president in 1997. Then Liberia exploded in a new fury of violent resistance to his rule, culminating in his fall from power and forced exile in 2003. There were many layers of more immediate and compelling local, ethnic and regional motives driving the cycle of conflicts. But it is also true that, during these long years of civil war, parties on all sides of the conflicts, at one time or another, hoped for, expected, or sought US intervention.[19] It could be hypothesized therefore that the prospect of US involvement was a common, albeit underlying, influence upon their decisions to fight.[20]

If the remote moral hazard suggested here did influence events, it stemmed from a vague yet long-standing American interest in the political affairs of that African state.[21] Victor LeVine's explanation for why the USA came "to acquire what everyone in the region (except perhaps most Americans) sees as a moral responsibility to save the Liberians" is suggestive:

> One reason is that the United States, which never had colonies in Africa, not only sent black American settlers to Liberia (15,386 between 1820 and 1899) but pretty much oversaw the creation of the Republic of Liberia (in 1847). During the next 150 years, the United States repeatedly intervened in Liberia to prevent political and economic collapses (Le Vine, 2003, p. B5).

From this vantage point the potential incentive would be not only remote but specific, because the longstanding US interest in Liberia is unique to Liberia. No other African groups would be encouraged to gamble on US support in the way Liberian groups have because no other African country has a similar "unique relationship" with the USA, based on "deep and longstanding ties" (quotes from Kansteiner, 2003). It is also interesting to note the role that accumulated negative precedents would play in building up the incentive: over the preceding 150 years the USA had, in Le Vine's words, "repeatedly intervened" in Liberia. This suggests that it would have been (and will continue to be) much harder for US policy makers to take effective action to remove the underlying perverse incentive, even though its baleful effects may be anticipated. Here again, then, we would have an instance of 'thin' moral hazard.

Contagious moral hazard (proximate cause and plural domain).   The empirical pattern to be explained here is a sudden spate of violent uprisings across political contexts. The moral hazard appears as a marked and common shift in the incentives facing the different groups, which immediately precedes the resort to violence by each of them. That shift in incentives could result directly from action taken by an intervenor, or indirectly from a structural change in the international balance of power—e.g. the collapse of the USSR—which signals a greater prospect that outsiders will underwrite or deflect the cost of internal revolts.[22]

One example of the former occurred in the aftermath of NATO military intervention in Kosovo in 1999. Shortly after NATO forces occupied the province, ethnic Albanian rebels in the Presevo Valley of Serbia proper, and in the neighbouring Republic of Macedonia, began to agitate and turn to violence (Ash, 2001). Groups within Montenegro also began to call more vehemently for political separation from Belgrade, and what is especially interesting is that the groups calling for separation were not all, or even mostly, ethnic Albanian. Two things are clear about the Presevo and Macedonia rebels. First, their respective grievances, although quite different, are longstanding ones.[23] Second, they were emboldened to seek remedy through violence by the advent of NATO occupation of Kosovo. Both uprisings, as Kuperman notes, "fizzled out" once it became clear that NATO not only would not support them, but indeed would oppose them (2004, p. 66). As the International Crisis Group put it: "NATO dashed rebel hopes by taking Belgrade's side" (2001b, p. ii).

This represents a compelling instance of 'thin' moral hazard. Before NATO went to war in Kosovo, Western leaders were aware of the dangers of emboldening Albanian rebels in Kosovo (Crawford, 2001). It is therefore not plausible that they failed to anticipate similar results elsewhere in the region. Although they did not intend to stoke more rebellion in the Balkans, they understood that their actions in Kosovo might do so. It is also clear that they did not seek to do so. Indeed, a purpose of the intervention was to suppress the spread of instability. Nevertheless, it was a risk they were prepared to take. So the perverse side-effect was anticipated but not intended. Finally, the case also illustrates how close proximity of the incentive to the perverse results, and the greater ability to foresee them, may allow leaders to make adjustments which reverse those consequences when they occur.

Pervasive moral hazard (remote cause and plural domain).   Here the hazardous incentive is a widespread and lurking background condition which inclines discontented groups to be more optimistic about the potential benefits of resorting to force. The observable consequences do not paint a coherent picture: the resulting rebellions occur sporadically, as local grievances accumulate, central governments weaken and perhaps the right pretexts present themselves. Precisely for this reason, we are hard pressed to produce a crisp empirical illustration. Because it is everywhere, we see it nowhere. It will have to suffice, therefore, to provide examples of this mode of explanation as it appears in arguments about moral hazard. Two come immediately to mind. The first comes from Kuperman's work, and the second comes from my own.

The Kuperman version boils down to an assertion of the causal force of a transnational 'norm' or 'regime'. This "intervention regime," he argues, "actually exacerbates some conflicts" (2004, p. 64). Elsewhere, he argues more forcefully that it does more, by posing to subordinate groups "a perverse incentive to initiate violent challenges against much stronger opponents in order to provoke a violent crackdown against their own people, in hopes of compelling sympathetic media attention, Western threats, and ultimately military intervention" (2003a, p. 58). The regime, in this line of argument, did not suddenly burst forth, but rather crept into existence after the end of the Cold War, and has been gaining ground ever since, through a combination of irresponsible rhetoric and occasional negative-precedent setting interventions (Kuperman, 2006; 2004; 2003a, p. 57). It reached something of an apex in December 2001, when "a distinguished international panel ... declared the existence of a 'Responsibility to Protect'—suggesting that the failure to intervene by those capable of doing so might even breach international law" (2004, p. 64).

A few points may be noted. First, the domain of moral hazard influence is truly plural—apparently including all fighting and non-fighting subordinate groups world-wide. Second, the first mover in the explanation—that is, the causer of the incentive-effect—is fuzzy, ranging from 'Western powers' at the most concrete end, to a 'regime' at the other, with 'sympathetic media' somewhere in between. This raises some hard methodological problems when it comes to testing the implied causal argument, but these will not be addressed here (see Crawford, 2004). It is also very hard to ground the un-intention condition of the moral hazard concept descriptively when the 'intender' is not well specified. Since at least some policy makers, as well as advocates of humanitarian intervention, do recognize that its precedents may encourage uprisings, it is best to see this as a problem of thin moral hazard.[24]

A somewhat different set of issues arises in an argument put forward by me, for the purposes of attacking the naïve notion that US 'global leadership' and 'forward engagement' reinforces regional stability and promotes peaceful change:

> Because the [USA] may significantly influence the outcome of many conflicts, that potential must be seen for what it is: something that, by looming so large, may encourage as well as discourage revisionism ... Because the benefits of enlisting US support in a war may be enormous, even the slim chance of doing so may goad a party to act provocatively, become inflexible in negotiations, or otherwise do things which make war more likely. In sum, forward US engagement may fuel disintegrative as well as integrative tendencies in world politics and 'jiggle loose' as many deadly conflicts as it knits back together (Crawford, 2003, p. 209).

The most obvious parallels between this and Kuperman's argument are the causal remoteness of the incentive-effect—it is a broad background condition shading rather than triggering others' decisions to use force—and the breadth of the scope and domain, which are very inclusive. The domain—regional antagonists—is certainly plural, including both states and sub-state groups world-wide. Consequently, the scope condition is also extremely broad, including both civil and international wars. It is fair to say that the breadth of these conditions makes it hard to conceive of a pattern of evidence sufficiently distinct to demonstrate the overall empirical consequences.

On the plus side, the source of the incentive is clearly identified—the USA. This makes it possible to pin down a number of the relevant conceptual issues. That many of the consequences are both unintended and unanticipated seems obvious, given the enormous indeterminacy implied by a policy of 'forward engagement'. If a kind of moral hazard is at work here, it is thicker rather than thinner. But that still leaves the question of whether any of these consequences are perverse, i.e. contrary to US interests. Unless we subscribe to the untenable premise that the US national interest is to preserve the status quo worldwide, on this score at least, the moral-hazard concept is not universally applicable here.

Finally, in both the examples above it is clear that the opportunities for achieving policy traction over the putative moral hazards are quite limited, at least in the short run. The causal force of a regime comes from an accumulation of precedents, which are not easily undone. To quell it would require a dramatic turn away from intervention on the part of the most powerful actors in the international system, and change in the way they justify the interventions they do ultimately undertake (i.e. in terms of sweeping international norms). Likewise, the US policy of forward engagement is a continuation of a long-established historical pattern that cannot be rewritten, involving many negative precedents, as well as reputation stakes, which can be gambled on by others. Furthermore, if the underlying impetus for US global engagement is less a matter of foreign policy choice, and more a function of the sheer 'energy' created by the preponderance of American power, curtailing the hazardous incentives it creates may have to await a fundamental diminution of that power disparity.[25]

Conclusions

We will conclude with key points regarding the concept of moral hazard and how it may be used in explanations of internal war. These do not purport to solve the controversies surrounding the moral hazard research programme. But, by keeping them in mind, scholars who use the concept can make more transparent and tractable arguments, and scholars who oppose them can mount more productive and revealing challenges.

1. The explanatory core of the moral hazard concept is perverse incentives. Negative precedents are a particular type of perverse incentive. You can have a moral hazard explanation without negative precedents, but you cannot have one without perverse incentives. Therefore, one question must always be answered in an empirical application of the concept—perverse relative to whose interest?
2. Because perverse incentives imply an influence relationship, the actor or actors creating the incentive should be identified. Only by doing so can we firmly establish that the incentive effects were perverse and unintended.
3. Empirical applications of the moral hazard concept should distinguish between the direct and indirect consequences of perverse incentives. Direct consequences appear in the behaviour of actors induced by the incentives. Indirect consequences appear in others' reactions (or anticipated reactions) to such behaviour.
4. Empirical applications of the moral hazard concept should distinguish between unintended perverse consequences that are anticipated and those that are unanticipated. In situations involving the former, there are likely to be serious debates over the intervenor's true interests, specifically questioning whether consequences can actually be considered perverse for the intervenor if it took action that knowingly caused them to occur.
5. Scholars should distinguish between 'thick' and 'thin' versions of moral hazard. Thin moral hazard occurs when intervenors create incentives that either: indirectly cause perverse consequences they do not intend and do not anticipate; or directly cause perverse consequences they do not intend but *do* anticipate. Thick moral hazard occurs when the intervenors' are truly 'thick': they create incentives that directly cause perverse consequences they neither intend nor anticipate.
6. Instances in which thick moral hazard is a proximate cause of conflict will be rare, because intervenors will rarely be so blind to the likely immediate consequences of their action. Much more frequently thin types of moral hazard will be the proximate cause of conflict. Accordingly, it will be easier to generalize about thin moral hazard than about thick moral hazard, which will not only be rare but anomalous.
7. Unanticipated consequences will play a larger role in plural domains and a smaller role in singular domains. In a singular domain, the effect of even a remote incentive is more likely to be understood, even if it cannot be altered. In a plural domain, by contrast, the effect of any incentive is harder for its creators to predict. The plural context thus implies more separation between the intervenors' intentions and the cumulative (and perverse) results it induces. Thus thin moral hazard in which perverse consequences are unanticipated—e.g. when intervention provokes states to commit genocide—is more likely to occur in plural domains. Conversely, thin moral hazard in which perverse consequences are not intended but *are* anticipated—e.g. when proximate threats to intervene induce rebellion—is more likely to occur in singular domains.
8. In any explanation involving moral hazard the question arises as to how much responsibility for the perverse consequences we can attribute to the policy makers in charge of the government(s) that raised expectations of intervention. The more proximate and singular the moral hazard incentive, the more ability to foresee, and perhaps control, the consequences we may impute to its authors. The more remote and plural the

moral hazard incentive, the less control and foresight we may impute to its authors, and the more the weight of responsibility for anticipating and adjusting to the consequences falls upon those who attempt to exploit it.

Acknowledgements

Earlier versions of this paper were presented at the Department of Political Science IR Workshop at Boston College, November 2004, the Annual Meeting of the American Political Science Association, September 2004 and the Georgetown University Workshop on Intervention, October 2003. Thanks for helpful feedback to: Orly Mishan, Jon Culp, Alexandre Provencher-Gravel, David Deese, Arman Grigorian, Don Hafner, Dennis Hale, Ron Hassner, Alan Kuperman, Robert Rauchhaus, Jack Snyder, Leslie Vinjamuri, Harrison Wagner, and Jon Western.

Notes

1. As a causal mechanism, moral hazard may produce the onset of war, or prolong it. This chapter will focus on the former role, although many of the points apply as well to the latter. See Crawford (2004).
2. A fuller discussion of normative issues appears in Crawford (2004). For an exhaustive cross-disciplinary study of the normative dimensions of the concept, see Baker (1996).
3. The close to Viner's passage is telling: "it was possible to picture [this] as a clash between the humane and hard-hearted". Similarly, Kuperman notes that "a policy of not intervening in cases of intentionally provoked genocide is open to criticism as being hard-hearted" (2003, p. 68). Although the poor laws debate obviously evoked the insurance–moral hazard connection, the term 'moral hazard' did not come into use until 30 years later, specifically in relation to private insurance rather than government welfare policies. See Baker (1996, p. 248, n. 44).
4. James D. Fearon (forthcoming) reinforces this traditional critique of self-determination. A melding of the negative precedent problems of appeasement and partition appears in relation to government responses to secessionist movements. Why do some governments absorb tremendous costs to crush breakaway rebellions on largely worthless territory? The most compelling answer is that they do so in order to avoid encouraging secessionist movements waiting elsewhere in the wings. This is the thrust of Walter (2003).
5. Nevertheless, Rauchhaus (2006) does not agree that the concept of moral hazard fits well with the empirical contours of the political problem.
6. It is essential to posit such revisionist motivations, because the prospect of protection against loss may have a very different effect on status quo seekers—that is, it may embolden them to take risks to preserve peace.
7. As I put it elsewhere, moral hazard "arises when you encourage others to do things against your interest with the prospect that you will bear the costs of their behavior" (Crawford, 2001, p. 504).
8. India's ambassador to the UN declared that India's intervention to "rescue the people of East Bengal" was motivated by "absolutely nothing but the purest of motives and the purest of intentions". Quoted in Franck and Rodley (1973, p. 276).
9. This calls to mind the principle of 'double effect' in just war theory. See Walzer (2000, p. 153). Thanks to Ron Hassner for pointing this out. On using the principle to think more broadly about the unintended consequences of foreign policy, see Jokela (2005).
10. Note, however, that Grigorian (2006) and Rauchhaus (2006) may disagree with this point; for them a moral hazard problem cannot exist if the intervenor is able to observe the perverse consequences of its policy, and is also able to alter the policy, but persists in it anyway.
11. According to the second edition of the *Oxford English Dictionary*, 'unwitting' unambiguously denotes "having no knowledge or cognizance of a particular fact, thing, etc.". Very close in meaning is 'inadvertence', which denotes "inattentive, negligent, heedless" persons, or actions "characterized by want of attention or taking notice; hence unintentional".
12. This is my extrapolation from Kuperman's larger argument.
13. According to Hugh Thomas (2001, pp. 328–329.), "apparently Franco did [not] know of" Mussolini's support for the failed rightist plot of 1934, but General Emelio Mola Vidal, the instigator of the part of the 1936 uprising that began *in Spain proper*, certainly did. Franco's half of the revolt started in Morocco.

14. This reasoning suggests the work of scholars who emphasize the necessary role of 'opportunity structures' in the decisions of aggrieved and mobilized groups to rebel. See McAdam (1982) and Tarrow (1994).

15. There is a challenge to the deductive logic in this line of argument, which starts with the observation that it assumes away the problem of misperceptions in real-time decision making. Thus, as Kuperman (personal communication) has pointed out, "one could argue the opposite—that distant causation is less likely to produce unintended consequences because policy makers previously will have had time to see the initial unanticipated consequences of the causal variable and to make mid-course corrections to avoid their repetition". The disagreement thus reduces to two larger disagreements about the prevalence of misperceptions. The first pertains to the relative proportion of misperceptions to accurate perceptions in general: how often do policy makers make choices based on inaccurate understandings of their situation? The second pertains to whether misperceptions are likely to be stronger and more prevalent in the near term or over the long run. The key work arguing for the high frequency and tenacity of misperceptions is Jervis (1976).

16. The 'scope' condition—the issue or behaviour influenced—has been made explicit throughout: that is, the propensity of the induced actors to rebel violently. The most thorough treatment of the need to specify scope, domain and other boundary conditions in power analysis is Baldwin (1989).

17. Kuperman notes that, "this was not the first time ... that the US [gave] false hope to Iraq's Kurds only to abandon them to Saddam's mercy" (2003a, p. 60, n. 22). The previous incident, which elicited Henry Kissinger's famous remark that "covert action should not be confused with missionary work", occurred in 1975 (Issacson, 1992, p. 564). In 1972, as a favour to the Shah of Iran, the USA began secretly arming the Kurds. Three years later, when Iran made amends with Iraq, the USA abandoned the Kurds, who were then demolished by Baghdad. The fact that in this case they had been summarily abandoned suggests, however, that it was not a precedent which encouraged them to rebel in 1991.

18. In a radio interview with Marvin Kalb (America Abroad Media, 2003), former Director of Central Intelligence Robert Gates, who served on the deputies committee which handled Iraq policy was asked: were "the Shiites in the South and the Kurds in the North...encouraged...to rise up against Saddam Hussein? Did you ever discuss coming to the immediate military help of these two groups?" Gates responded: "The President's encouragement had been an expression of hope that the Iraqi people would take action to depose Saddam Hussein. I don't recall that the Kurds or the Shia were specifically incited to rise up themselves. I think that in the back of our minds our hope had never been, or our belief had never been, that that the Kurds or the Shia could get rid of Saddam. It was the Generals that we anticipated would get rid of him. And frankly the uprisings gave Saddam the pretext for trying to hold the military together while he put them down."

19. The International Crisis Group (2003: pp. i, 14) reported that the anti-Taylor factions in the fighting of 2003 had received at least "tacit backing" from the US government in their efforts to depose him. Yet, during the same period, Taylor was calling for US intervention to stop the fighting and broker a transfer of power under government elections. For example, on 8 July, in a CNN interview, Taylor called for US intervention to break the siege of Monrovia by rebel forces: "Some of us feel that you owe it to this country, because we've been by you and we continue to stand by you" (CNN.com Transcripts, 2003). In 1990 Taylor's foe Samuel Doe similarly appealed to Washington for support: "We implore you to come help your stepchildren who are in danger of losing their lives and their freedom" (quoted in Pham, 2004).

20. I have not found evidence of rebel decision making to support this hypothesis, so it must be considered valid only as an illustration of a potential explanation based on remote and singular moral hazard.

21. The USA did make explicit statements suggesting that it might intervene in the summer of 2003, but these came much too late to explain the rebels' decisions to fight in the first place.

22. Thanks to Alan Kuperman for calling attention to the potential for structural change to trigger proximate and plural consequences.

23. "For many years", notes the International Crisis Group, "observers of the Balkans had expected trouble to break out in Macedonia before Kosovo erupted rather than afterwards" (2001a, p. 9). See also International Crisis Group (2001b, p. 2) and Daalder (2000).

24. However, if one were to argue that a direct effect of the humanitarian intervention regime is to cause governments (anticipating its emboldening effect on subordinate groups) pre-emptively to inflict genocide on potential challengers, you would have a full-fledged instance of thick moral hazard. This causal mechanism is noted in Wagner (2006)—although he does not consider it a moral hazard phenomenon—and discussed at length in Bloom (1999).

25. On the idea that "US power creates its own foreign policy energy", see Posen (2004, p. 8).

References

America Abroad Media (2003) Iraq: the context of a crisis, Segment 2, 18 February, audio available online at: http://www.americaabroadmedia.org/explore-details.php?id=48.

Ash, T. G. (2001) Is there a good terrorist?, *New York Review of Books*, 29 November.

Baert, P. (1991) Unintended consequences: a typology and hypotheses, *International Sociology*, 6(2), pp. 201–210.

Baker, T. (1996) On the genealogy of moral hazard, *Texas Law Review*, 75(2), pp. 237–292.

Baldwin, D. A. (1989) *Paradoxes of Power* (New York: Blackwell).

Bernard, L. L. (1972) *War and Its Causes* (New York: Garland).

Blechman, B.M. & Kaplan, S. S. (1978) *Force Without War* (Washington, DC: Brookings Institution).

Bloom, M. M. (1999) Failures of intervention: the unintended consequences of mixed messages and the exacerbation of ethnic conflict, PhD thesis, Columbia University.

Brodie, B. (1973) *War and Politics* (New York: Macmillan).

Carr, E. H. (1942) *Conditions of Peace* (New York: Macmillan).

CNN.com Transcripts (2003) Live from the headlines: Liberian president looks toward the future, 8 July, available online at: http://cnnstudentnews.cnn.com/TRANSCRIPTS/0307/08/se.14.html

Crawford, T.W. (1998)Why minimum force won't work: doctrine and deterrence in Bosnia and beyond, *Global Governance*, 4(2), pp. 235–256.

Crawford, T. W. (2001) Pivotal deterrence and the Kosovo war: why the Holbrooke Agreement failed, *Political Science Quarterly*, 116(4), pp. 499–523.

Crawford, T. W. (2003) *Pivotal Deterrence: Third-Party Statecraft and the Pursuit of Peace* (Ithaca, NY: Cornell University Press).

Crawford, T. W. (2004) Moral hazard causal arguments, paper prepared for delivery at the 2004 Annual Meeting of the American Political Science Association.

Daalder, I. (2000) Nip Balkan's bloody spring in the bud, *Newsday*, 21 March.

Dahl, R. A. (1984) *Modern Political Analysis* (Englewood Cliffs, NJ: Prentice-Hall).

David, S. (1997) Internal war: causes and cures, *World Politics*, 49(4), pp. 552–576.

DeConde, A. (1978) *A History of American Foreign Policy* (New York: Charles Scribner's Sons).

Dombrowski, P. & Payne, R. (2003) Global debate and the limits of the Bush Doctrine, *International Studies Perspectives*, 4(4), pp. 395–408.

Elster, J. (1989) *Nuts and Bolts for the Social Sciences* (New York: Cambridge University Press).

Fearon, J. D. (forthcoming) Separatist wars, partition, and world order, *Security Studies*.

Franck, T. M. & Rodley, N. S. (1973) After Bangladesh: the law of humanitarian intervention by military force, *American Journal of International Law*, 67(2), pp. 275–305.

Grigorian, A. (2006) Third-party intervention and escalation in Kosovo: does moral hazard explain it? in: T.W. Crawford and A.J. Kuperman (Eds.), *Gambling on Humanitarian Intervention* (London: Routledge).

Heisbourg, F. (2003) A work in progress: the Bush Doctrine and its consequences, *Washington Quarterly*, 26(2), pp. 75–88.

International Crisis Group (2001a) *The Macedonian Question: Reform or Rebellion*, ICG Balkans Report No. 109, 5 April, available online at: http://www.icg.org/home/index.cfm?id=1704&l=1.

International Crisis Group (2001b) *Peace in Presevo: Quick Fix or Long Term Solution*, ICG Balkans Report No. 116, 10 August, available online at: http://www.icg.org/home/index.cfm?id=1723&l=1.

International Crisis Group (2003) *Liberia: Security Challenges*, ICG Africa Report No. 71, 3 November, available online at: http://www.icg.org/home/index.cfm?id=2344&l=1.

Issacson, W. (1992) *Kissinger* (New York: Simon & Schuster).

Jatras, J. G. (2000) NATO's myths and bogus justifications for intervention, in: T.G. Carpenter (Ed.), *NATO's Empty Victory: A Post-Mortem on the Balkan War*, pp. 21–29 (Washington, DC: CATO Institute).

Jervis, R. (1976) *Perception and Misperception in International Politics* (Princeton, NJ: Princeton University Press).

Jervis, R. (1989) *The Meaning of the Nuclear Revolution: Statecraft and the Prospect of Armageddon* (Ithaca, NY: Cornell University Press).

Jervis, R. (1997) *System Effects* (Princeton, NJ: Princeton University Press).

Jokela, M. (2005) Ethical dimensions of the unintended consequences of foreign policy, paper presented at the 46th Annual Convention of the International Studies Association, 1–5 March 2005, Honolulu, HI.

Kansteiner, W. H. (2003) Assistant Secretary of State for African Affairs, Testimony to House Committee on International Relations Subcommittee on Africa, 2 October 2003, available online at: http://www.state.gov/p/af/rls/rm/24839.htm.

Kuperman, A. J. (1996) The other lesson of Rwanda: sometimes mediators do more harm than good, *SAIS Review*, 16(1), pp. 221–240.

Kuperman, A. J. (2003a) Transnational causes of genocide, or how the West exacerbates ethnic conflict, in: R. G. C. Thomas (Ed.), *Yugoslavia Unraveled: Sovereignty, Self-Determination, Intervention*, pp. 55–85 (Lanham, MD: Lexington Books).

Kuperman, A. J. (2003b) Suffering, *The National Interest*, 71, pp. 136–141.

Kuperman, A. J. (2004) Humanitarian hazard: revisiting doctrines of intervention, *Harvard International Review*, 26(1), pp. 64–68.

Kuperman, A. J. (2006) Suicidal rebellions and the moral hazard of humanitarian intervention, in: T.W. Crawford and A.J. Kuperman (Eds.), *Gambling on Humanitarian Intervention* (London: Routledge).

Le Vine, V. T. (2003) Liberia commentary: past US involvement may require help today, *St. Louis Dispatch*, 20 July.

Lebow, R. N. (1981) *Between Peace and War: The Nature of International Crises* (Baltimore, MD: Johns Hopkins University Press).

Lischer, S. K. (2003) Collateral damage: humanitarian assistance as a cause of conflict, *International Security*, 28(1), pp. 79–109.

McAdam, D. (1982) *Political Process and the Development of Black Insurgency, 1930–1970* (Chicago: University of Chicago Press).

Merton, R. (1936) The unanticipated consequences of purposive social action, American Sociological Review, 1(6), pp. 894–904.

Oppenheim, F. (1975) The language of political inquiry: problems of clarification, in: F.I. Greenstein & N.W. Polsby (Eds), *Handbook of Political Science*, Vol. 1, ch. 5 (Reading, MA: Addison-Wesley).

Oxford English Dictionary (1989) Second edition (Oxford: Oxford University Press).

Pham, J. P. (2004) Déjà vu in Port-Au-Prince, *In the National Interest*, 3 March, available online at: http://www.inthenationalinterest.com/Articles/Vol3Issue9/Vol3Issue9Pham.html

Posen, B. (2004) ESDP and the structure of world power, *The International Spectator*, 44(1), pp. 5–17.

Price, J. (2001) *Thucydides and Internal War* (Cambridge: Cambridge University Press).

Rauchhaus, R. (2000) Third party intervention in militarized disputes: *primum non nocere*, PhD thesis, University of California Berkeley.

Rauchhaus, R. (2003) letter to author, 10 June.

Rauchhaus, R. (2006) Humanitarian intervention, conflict management and the application and misapplication of moral hazard theory, in: T.W. Crawford and A.J. Kuperman (Eds.), *Gambling on Humanitarian Intervention* (London: Routledge).

Record, J. (2003) The Bush Doctrine and the war with Iraq, *Parameters*, 33(1), pp. 4–21.

Rowlands, D. & Carment, D. (1998) Moral hazard and conflict intervention, in: M. Wolfson (Ed.), *The Political Economy of War and Peace*, pp. 267–285 (Boston, MA: Kluwer).

Salerno, R. M. (2002) *Vital Crossroads: Mediterranean Origins of the Second World War, 1935–1940* (Ithaca, NY: Cornell University Press).

Sambanis, N. (2000) Partition as a solution to ethnic war, *World Politics*, 52(4), pp. 437–83.

Schroeder, P.W. (2002) Iraq: the case against preemptive war, *American Conservative Magazine*, October 21, available online at: http://www.amconmag.com/2002_10_21/iraq.html

Sontag, R. J. (1971) *A Broken World, 1919–1939* (New York: Harper & Row).

Snyder, G. (1984) The security dilemma in alliance politics, *World Politics*, 36(4), pp. 461–495.

Tarrow, S. (1994) *Power in Movement: Social Movements, Collective Action, and Politics* (New York: Cambridge University Press).

Thomas, H. (2001) *The Spanish Civil War* (New York: The Modern Library).

Thucydides (1982) *The Peloponnesian War* (New York: Random House).

Viner, J. (1940) The short view and the long in economic policy, *American Economic Review*, 30(1), pp. 1–15.

Wagner, R. H. (2006) The hazards of thinking about moral hazard, in: T.W. Crawford and A.J. Kuperman (Eds.), *Gambling on Humanitarian Intervention* (London: Routledge).

Walter, B. F. (2003) Explaining the intractability of territorial conflict, *International Studies Review*, 5(4), pp. 137–153.

Waltz, K. N. (1959) *Man, the State, and War* (New York: Columbia University Press).

Walzer, M. (2000) *Just and Unjust Wars* (New York: Basic Books).

Wolfers, A (1945) Conflict and compromise at San Francisco, Memorandum Number 16, Yale Institute of International Studies, 24 April.

Wohlstetter, A. (1959) The delicate balance of terror, *Foreign Affairs*, 37(2), pp. 211–234.

Wright, Q. (1935) *Causes of War and the Conditions of Peace* (New York: Longmans, Green).

Wright, Q. (1965) *A Study of War*, (Chicago: University of Chicago Press).

Third-party Intervention and Escalation in Kosovo: Does Moral Hazard Explain It?

ARMAN GRIGORIAN

The claim that inaction by third parties is the most important permissive cause of the violence that states commit against minorities remains the prevalent view in the Western discourse on interventions. The outdated and morally indefensible norm of sovereignty makes it possible for states to perpetrate horrible crimes against their citizens, the familiar argument goes, and therefore the norm must be replaced by one obligating, or at least allowing, the international community to intervene to protect the victims of such violence. It is not an unchallenged view anymore, however. Over the past few years it has come under increased scrutiny and criticism. A number of studies has confronted the common wisdom with the fact that conflicts between states and minorities often take a turn for the worse after third parties become involved.

Several competing arguments have emerged to explain this phenomenon. One of the most interesting and increasingly popular among them is based on the logic of moral hazard (Rowlands & Carment, 1998; Crawford, 2001; Kuperman, 2002; Kuperman, 2003). Stated briefly, its proponents claim that threats of third-party intervention to protect minorities against state-sponsored violence provide minorities with perverse incentives to behave recklessly, and even to provoke the very violence that third parties were trying to protect the minority from. The argument is especially popular in studies of the conflict in Kosovo, the most intensely debated case of third-party intervention in the 1990s, and one which seems to provide abundant evidence of reckless and provocative behaviour by the Kosovo Albanians, or at least the insurgents known as the Kosovo Liberation Army (KLA) acting on their behalf (Jatras, 2000, pp. 23–24; Daalder & O'Hanlon, 2000, pp. 84–89; Crawford, 2001; Kuperman, 2003; Thomas, 2003, pp. 16–18).[1]

This argument is a major improvement on the conventional wisdom both as a general theory of violence committed by states against minorities, and as an explanation of what transpired in Kosovo. Its proponents should be congratulated for one thing in particular. They correctly reject the misguided assumption that violence against minorities is simply apolitical barbarism by certain kinds of states, and instead frame the issue as a problem of bargaining between states and minorities. They see the problem as one of strategic interaction, in other words, and treat minorities as strategic actors in their own right, rather than mere objects of violence. The argument is not entirely free of problems, however. It does not explain the target-state's decision calculus satisfactorily, for example. While it is more than plausible that a threat of intervention would affect the bargaining behaviour of the minority, it is implausible that that threat would not be incorporated into the target-state's calculus as well. How exactly the state's calculus is affected by such threats, however, is left largely unaccounted for in this literature. There are also certain inconsistencies in this literature regarding the credibility of third-party threats to intervene. For instance, if third-party threats lack credibility, they should not have any appreciable effect either on the minority's or the target-state's behaviour. Some authors argue, however, that these threats lack credibility *and* that they lead to escalated violence.

There are also certain empirical claims made on behalf of this theory, including some in the context of Kosovo, that stretch the concept of moral hazard beyond the breaking point. Specifically, while the moral hazard argument may explain certain aspects and events of the Kosovo tragedy in the period between the rise of the KLA in 1996 and the escalation of tensions in January 1999 after the massacre of Kosovo Albanians in Racak, it has difficulties explaining others. For instance, the theory cannot explain why the USA was unable to threaten the KLA with abandonment throughout this period, which is something it *must* explain. What happened after the Racak massacre is even more puzzling if moral hazard is our analytical lens. The US ultimatum at Rambouillet, NATO's decision to bomb Serbia and the Serbian decision to force the ethnic Albanians out of Kosovo are particularly difficult to reconcile with the moral hazard logic.

In what follows, I will try to substantiate these criticisms in more detail. I will provide a more extensive analysis of the moral hazard argument, as well as discuss the evidence from Kosovo in light of that analysis. I will also propose an alternative theoretical framework, which I think more adequately captures both the strategic dynamic that characterizes third-party interventions in general, and which I believe better fits the evidence from Kosovo. Briefly, I will argue that incomplete information about Milosevic's cost-tolerance and capacity for barbarity, and about NATO's willingness to escalate the intervention into a ground war if Milosevic opted for a 'final solution', was what produced the horror in Kosovo in the spring of 1999.

Threats of Intervention and Moral Hazard

Life is full of risks, which people, as well as organizations and groups, constantly try to reduce. Risk reduction has obvious benefits for the carrier of the risk, but it can also be socially desirable and Pareto optimal. An individual who buys insurance makes sure that he or she will be compensated if the risk materializes, in return for a fee to the insurance provider, which benefits both the insurer and the insured. Certain indispensable institutions and transactions would not even be possible if the risks for them could not be reduced. Banks, for example, might not exist if they were not insured against excessive defaulted loans. Surgeons would stop performing difficult and high-risk surgery if they were not insured against lawsuits for making errors. There are countless similar examples demonstrating the virtues of reduced risks.

The effects of risk reduction, however, are non-linear. All else does not remain equal when risks are reduced. As Prajit Dutta puts it, "if you don't have comprehensive insurance on your car you may think twice about parking right in front of the rowdiest downtown bar on a Friday night" (Dutta, 1999, p. 293). Insurance, in other words, affects not just one's risks, but also the likelihood of running them—increasing the cost to the insurer. The level of insurance and the incentives for prudence are thus in an inverse relationship, and that is the essence of the phenomenon known as 'moral hazard'.

It should be clear even from this very brief description how moral hazard can be relevant to interventions. By threatening to intervene to protect minorities if they are subjected to violence, third parties provide minorities with perverse incentives to play hardball with the host state or even to provoke the very violence that third parties were trying to prevent. This may be true, but there seems to be an obvious solution to this problem. Third parties can make their threats conditional on the minority's responsible behaviour. They can simply threaten the minority with abandonment if it behaves recklessly or if it initiates the violence itself. In one of the first systematic applications of the moral hazard logic to third-party interventions, however, Rowlands and Carment argue that the threat to abandon the minority may not be credible for two reasons. First, the third party may not be able to prove 'breach of contract'. More specifically, it may not always be easy to determine the identity of the initiator of violence. Second, if we relax the assumption that the minority is a unitary actor, another problem arises. Even if the third party is able to establish that members of the minority group instigated the violence, it may not be possible to separate the instigators from the group as a whole, refusing protection only to the instigators while extending it to the innocent non-combatants, if the state retaliates in an indiscriminate manner. The identity of the initiator, therefore, may be irrelevant (Rowlands & Carment, 1998, p. 271). The third party, in other words, may simply be entrapped by certain members of the victim group. Alan Kuperman adds a third and related reason: the Western media usually focus on the plight of the victims, and the momentum built in favour of the 'victim group' becomes impossible to reverse regardless of who bears responsibility for it (Kuperman, 2002, p. 377). This is the so-called 'CNN effect'.[2]

This is a plausible and also a very elegant argument. It highlights important questions and problems usually ignored by many proponents of humanitarian intervention, who tend to see deterring violence, stopping violence, or failing to do either as the only possible consequences of third-party intervention. It demonstrates clearly that quite a bit of strategic interaction accompanies such violence, and that threats of intervention can have undesirable effects on the bargaining calculations of oppressed or threatened minorities. A number of questions, however, remain unanswered.

First, even if moral hazard explains why it may be *rational* for minorities to behave more provocatively as a result of such threats, it does not explain why the escalated violence should be the *equilibrium* outcome. Minorities may certainly acquire incentives to provoke violence as a consequence of threats of intervention to protect them, but why should the states that are potential targets of intervention be provoked? In fact, if the state and the minority have the same estimate regarding the likelihood of intervention, which is precisely what they should have if we are talking about *public* threats, the minority's recklessness should be proportionally compensated by the increased flexibility and caution on the part of the state. As Rupen Cetinyan has correctly observed, threats of third-party intervention should affect the terms and not the likelihood of peaceful settlements in state–minority disputes (Cetinyan, 2002, p. 647).[3] If, on the other hand, we are dealing not with *public threats*, but *private promises* of intervention to the minority, then the state's behaviour need not become proportionally moderate and cautious. The problem is that this scenario has little to do with moral hazard.

Second, even if we relaxed certain overly restrictive assumptions and allowed a violent state response to minority provocation, say, because not responding would be costly for the government domestically, it is not clear why in some cases the response acquires genocidal proportions. In one of his articles Kuperman argues that states ('dominant groups' in his terminology) retaliate against provocations with mass expulsion and genocide in order to remove a threat before the West intervenes (Kuperman, 2002, p. 57). This claim is interesting, but problematic, because it requires an explanation of why minorities and third parties fail to anticipate such a response.

Third, even if the expectations of intervention are not false, and abandoning the minority is not an option, moral hazard is not an insurmountable problem. Third parties can simply refuse to endorse the minority's political demands even as they promise physical protection. In particular, they can, and more often than not do, refuse to recognize rebellious minorities as independent states, which is frequently the political end such minorities pursue. This may be the reason why the ratio of actual to potential ethnic rebellions is in fact quite small.[4]

The norm against secessionism, however, is not adhered to consistently. There have been cases where third parties have encouraged minorities and endorsed their demands. And this brings us to the fourth point. Cases where the minority toughened its position in response to such encouragement should not count as confirming evidence for the moral hazard theory. The Bosnian Muslims' refusal to sign a deal with the Serbs, worked out by the Europeans in 1992 following the advice from the US ambassador to that effect,[5] is not a case of moral hazard. It would be if the Bosnian Muslims had adopted the position they did *despite* American warnings not to do so. There is some evidence of the USA discouraging the Kosovo Albanians from assuming a tougher bargaining stance against Belgrade in some periods of that conflict, so the existence of moral hazard here is definitely more plausible. As I will demonstrate below, however, statements and acts by the USA that discouraged tough and provocative behaviour by Kosovo Albanians were overwhelmed by statements and acts that encouraged such behaviour.

Finally, the moral hazard argument may have a problem of selection bias. More specifically, we may be dealing with a case of systematically selecting observations on the dependent variable. Every case of escalation studied by the proponents of this approach is traced back to a minority's optimism regarding third-party intervention and its actions based on that optimism. Cases where similarly optimistic minorities behaved differently, therefore, have slipped through this methodological crack.[6] Kosovo Albanians could not have been more optimistic about external intervention in the case of a violent state crackdown than the Hungarians of Vojvodina, the Russian communities in the Baltic states, the Turks in Bulgaria, or Armenians in Georgia. Yet in these and many other cases where minorities could have reasonably expected intervention in the case of violence against them, they did not do what the moral hazard theory would have us expect. This is not meant as a suggestion that moral hazard is never a problem. It almost certainly is in some cases. At a minimum, however, the argument is indeterminate as it stands. To explain why some optimistic minorities behave provocatively, while others do not, or even why the same minority shifts its behaviour without a shift in third-party behaviour,[7] the proponents of the theory must identify variables that systematically interact with moral hazard, affecting its intensity.

In sum, while this theory has been a major step forward in the study of third-party interventions, there are still some open questions about its validity and applicability. The record of the theory is decidedly mixed even in Kosovo, which has been a particularly popular case for the proponents of the theory, and to which I will now turn.

What Happened in Kosovo? Just the Facts

The standard account of what happened in Kosovo in spring 1999, which is *not* the moral-hazard account, is well known. Slobodan Milosevic, who was a Serbian communist turned hypernationalist, decided to expel the Kosovo Albanians *en masse*, which was the natural culmination of a decade-long rampage of Serbian nationalism aimed at creating an ethnically pure Greater Serbia. There was nothing terribly surprising about this latest case of Serbian barbarism, given their earlier behaviour in the wars with the Croats and the Bosnian Muslims. What Milosevic and his underlings did in 1999 was simply the predictable last chapter of the decade-long history of genocide and ethnic cleansing unleashed by them. If third parties can be held responsible for anything, the argument goes, it is for having been too weak-kneed with Milosevic and the Serbs for too long. As far as the intervention in 1999 is concerned, the USA and its allies launched it in response to an escalating campaign of persecution. The intervention thwarted the plan of Milosevic and his fellow Serbian nationalists to remove Albanians from Kosovo, which was their plan all along and was going to be put into action sooner or later.[8]

This oversimplified and factually suspect account,[9] although still very popular, has come under criticism from a number of scholars, including the proponents of the moral-hazard school, who have tried to draw attention in particular to the provocative behavior of the KLA. They have also argued that the KLA's behaviour had much to do with its optimism regarding third-party intervention if the Serbs responded violently to their provocations. Before turning to their analysis of the evidence, we should establish some basic chronology of events.

Recent conflict between Serbs and Albanians in Kosovo was but the latest round in a long history. Political unrest has been a periodic problem in Kosovo throughout the history of post-World War II Yugoslavia. For the most part the Yugoslav system was able to manage the 'Kosovo problem' through a combination of carrots and sticks, but the underlying discontent, which had much to do with Kosovo's particularly abysmal economic situation and its status as part of Serbia rather than as a federal republic, was never completely removed. This discontent boiled over into fairly serious violence in 1981, which seems to have been a turning point. A student demonstration, which demanded improved living conditions at the Pristina University, quickly snowballed into riots, involving attacks on Kosovo's Serb population. The federal government responded by sending troops to Kosovo to suppress the riots. Order was restored eventually, but the tension in and around Kosovo was not quelled (Vickers, 1998, pp. 197–202). Kosovo Albanian nationalism was actually hardened by the riots and the federal government's heavy-handed response. Another even more ominous consequence of these developments was the weakening of the Serbian commitment to the idea of 'Yugoslavism'.[10] There were more and more open expressions of Serbian nationalism, which was partially fuelled by the Serbian anger over the maltreatment of Kosovo's Serbs.[11]

By 1983 the atmosphere of the Kosovo situation had become frenzied, with Serbs complaining not only about the harassment that was forcing Kosovo's Serbs out, but openly blaming the state welfare policy, which, according to them, encouraged a high Albanian birthrate. By 1985 the Serbian anger over this situation manifested itself as a movement supported by the Serbian Orthodox Church. Soon the Serbs and Montenegrins that had left Kosovo and moved to other parts of Serbia organized the so-called Kosovo Committee. This committee organized regular demonstrations and petition drives against the mistreatment of Kosovo's Slavs. On 15 January 1986, the journal *Knjizhevne Novine* published a petition signed by 2000 Serbs living in Kosovo denouncing Albanian nationalism (Vickers, 1998, p. 221). The most important event in this period, however, was the leaking of a draft secret memorandum on the general condition of Serbs in Yugoslavia by the Serbian Academy of Sciences and Arts. This document summarized the oppositional, nationalist narrative of Serbian grievances, giving it added legitimacy and weight because of the immense prestige of the institution where it had been prepared. The plight of Kosovo's Serbs was not the only focus of the document, but it received particular attention. The document called for policies that would reverse the demographic trend in Kosovo and for reduction of Kosovo's autonomous status, among other things, and went as far as calling what was happening to the Serbs 'genocide' (Vickers, 1998, pp. 222–223; Judah, 2002, pp. 49–50). Throughout this time the federal government also maintained a heavy security presence in Kosovo, with military checkpoints, secret agents, and trials of Albanians for crimes such as possession of nationalist literature.

This was the political atmosphere that elevated Slobodan Milosevic from a relatively little known party apparatchik into national prominence. On a trip to Kosovo, where he was sent to calm passions in April 1987, he delivered a speech in front of a large crowd of local Serbs in Kosovo Polje—an event that many consider to have been a turning point not just for Kosovo, but for Yugoslavia as a whole. Addressing the crowd, which had clashed with the police, he said that no one should dare beat them, and promised to address their grievances (Auerswald & Auerswald, 2000, pp. 1–4). This event arguably paved the way for Milosevic's rise to the leadership of the Serbian Communist Party. He seems to have realized here that the energy of pent-up Serbian anger and nationalism was far more promising political material than the old and tired slogans of communist brotherhood, and accordingly changed his rhetoric.

A few months after the events in Kosovo Polje the head of the Belgrade League of Communists, Dragisa Pavlovic, warned against the dangers of Serbian nationalism and publicly accused Milosevic of "revanchism against Albanians" (Auerswald & Auerswald, 2000, p. 2). By now, however, Milosevic had become powerful enough to have Pavlovic removed. In November 1988, after fully consolidating his grip over the Serbian Communist Party, Milosevic also had the highest ranking officials of Kosovo's League of Communists removed and replaced by people loyal to him. This triggered protests in Kosovo, which eventually grew into a general strike in February 1989, paralyzing the normal life of the province. In response, Milosevic had Azem Vlasi, who was one of the ousted leaders of Kosovo's League of Communists, arrested. In addition, on 28 September the Serbian Assembly approved a new constitution, which downgraded the autonomous status of both Kosovo and Vojvodina granted to them in 1974.

The Kosovo Albanians, for their part, held a referendum organized by the members of the Kosovo Assembly that earlier had been officially disbanded, and voted overwhelmingly for independence for the province. In May 1992 Kosovo Albanians also held elections for a parliament and a president, and elected Ibrahim Rugova as their leader. Serbians and the Kosovo Albanians soon settled into an uneasy and tense stalemate characterized by a tight and repressive Serbian policy in Kosovo and an uncompromising Albanian demand for independence. Large-scale violence was avoided, however, despite high tensions and political positions that were very hard to reconcile. This was partly a result of the Albanians having been successfully disarmed, and partly because Rugova was a pacifist, despite his political maximalism.

This equilibrium was maintained until the Dayton accords of 1995, which ended the war in Bosnia, and the subsequent arrival of the KLA on the political scene.[12] The KLA had decided that it was time to jettison Rugova's strategy of pacifism, which it argued had achieved very little. It started with sporadic attacks in 1996 and, by 1997, the KLA campaign had grown into a full-scale insurgency, which became possible also as a result of the political chaos in neighbouring Albania, where it became much easier for the KLA to get weapons.

The situation started deteriorating very fast in spring 1998. After the assassination of four Serbian policemen by the KLA on 28 February, Serbia retaliated with a crackdown. The crackdown itself triggered protests in Pristina, which the Serbian police responded to with massive use of force. In the meantime, Albanians held elections, and Rugova's party—the Democratic League of Kosova (LDK)—surprisingly won by a large margin. The KLA, however, boycotted the election. Shortly after the elections Rugova and Milosevic sat down to negotiate, thanks to the efforts of the so-called Contact Group, which included the USA, UK, Germany, France, Italy and Russia. Negotiations were held while violence continued, which Rugova considered unacceptable. In the end he walked out of the negotiations and declared that full independence for Kosovo was the only acceptable solution.

Hopes for a peaceful resolution were revived on 16 June 1998, when, as a result of Russian mediation, Milosevic signalled a willingness to make concessions on restoring Kosovo's autonomy, to allow access for foreign diplomats and international organizations to Kosovo, and to pull the Serbian police out of Kosovo. The ensuing shuttle diplomacy by Richard Holbrooke and a Russian representative to get this process on track failed completely, however, because the Kosovo Albanians refused to negotiate. By now, the KLA was the more powerful of the two main Albanian political organizations in Kosovo, and its opposition to the negotiations meant that there would not be any.

The Kosovo Albanian intransigence soon reached a point where even NATO started to become exasperated. Wesley Clark, the Supreme Allied Commander in Europe, even made some vague threats against the KLA. The Contact Group also announced that it would go after the KLA's funding. Most importantly, and most interestingly, NATO stood by and allowed a Serbian offensive against the KLA (Crawford, 2001, p. 509). These developments soon bore fruit. The LDK, which had regained its prominence as a result of the KLA's troubles on the battlefield, returned to the negotiating table. It not only restarted negotiations, but also dropped its insistence on outright independence and agreed to a plan that would grant Kosovo a status within the Federal Republic of Yugoslavia similar to Serbia and Montenegro (Weller, 1999, Vol. 1, p. 22). Something very strange happened soon after, however. NATO's tune changed quite dramatically, and it shifted the pressure back onto Belgrade. On 23 September the Security Council passed Resolution 1199 (UNSCR 1199), which condemned violence on both sides. But soon afterwards Belgrade became the main target of criticisms and threats. Shortly after the adoption of the resolution, the North Atlantic Council authorized General Clark to assemble a force for use in Kosovo. On 1 October the US Defense Secretary, William Cohen, announced that NATO could start bombing Serbia in two weeks, and on 13 October the North Atlantic Council ordered air strikes within 96 hours if Serbia did not comply with UNSCR 1199. Milosevic did comply, and on 13 October the so-called Holbrooke Agreement was announced. Milosevic agreed to withdraw the Serbian police from Kosovo. He also agreed to allow overflight rights for NATO aircraft so that his compliance could be verified. What he got in return was an assurance from General Clark and his deputy, Klaus Naumann, that NATO would not allow the KLA to exploit the Serbian withdrawal. To bolster this assurance, Secretary of State Albright declared: "There should be no attempt to take military advantage of the Serb pullback" (Albright, in Crawford, 2001, p. 512).

This commitment, however, was not honoured. The KLA did exploit the Serbian withdrawal. The Holbrooke Agreement failed, and the same pattern of KLA hit-and-run attacks and Serbian retaliation resumed, this time with more intense violence than before. The Western media and officials continued to blame the Serbs, although some of these officials privately and not so privately acknowledged that the KLA was responsible for this latest round of fighting (Crawford, 2001, p. 512). The West also tried to revive the negotiations without much success, because the KLA had again become the more powerful of the Kosovo Albanian organizations, and the LDK had accordingly hardened its position, again insisting on outright independence. Meanwhile, the fighting continued, and on 15 January 1999 something happened that galvanized the Contact Group into renewed pressure to resume negotiations. That something was the massacre of 45 Kosovo Albanians in a town called Racak. This event also refocused the blame for what was happening in Kosovo firmly on the Serbs. Soon after the massacre the Contact Group forced the warring parties to agree to negotiations at Rambouillet, France.

What took place at Rambouillet, however, were not negotiations. Belgrade was given an ultimatum according to which it was to surrender sovereignty over Kosovo for an interim period of three years. After this interim period Kosovo's status would be determined through a referendum (Auerswald & Auerswald, 2000, p. 590). The outcome of the referendum was a forgone conclusion, of course, which means that the USA basically endorsed the maximum Albanian demand, the three-year interim period being the only difference. The ultimatum also contained the following curious annex:

> NATO personnel shall enjoy, together with their vehicles, vessels, aircraft and equipment, free and unrestricted access throughout the FRY [Federal Republic of

Yugoslavia] including associated airspace and territorial waters. This shall include, but not be limited to, the right of bivouac, maneuver, billet, and utilization of any areas or facilities as required for support, training, and operations. (Auerswald & Auerswald, 2000, p. 588)

The Serbs rejected the ultimatum. Soon afterwards, on 24 March, NATO launched an air campaign against Serbia against which Belgrade retaliated with a massive campaign of ethnic cleansing in Kosovo; it was eventually reversed after Milosevic decided to settle 11 weeks into the bombing campaign.

Was Moral Hazard the Problem?

What does the preceding description of events tell us about the causes of escalation in Kosovo in the winter of 1998–99, and particularly about the causes of the attempted ethnic cleansing in March–May of 1999? Does history support the moral-hazard argument? There are indeed indisputable elements of moral hazard in this story, demonstrated both by certain events and by some statements of the participants in these events.

Kuperman, for instance, quotes a shocking statement by a certain KLA negotiator that could have been copied from a textbook on moral hazard. This negotiator is quoted as follows: "The more civilians were killed, the chances of international intervention became bigger, and the KLA of course realized that" (Kuperman, 2003, p. 68). There is some evidence that the USA tried to isolate the KLA or pressure it to moderate its behaviour on a number of occasions without much success. The USA seemed unable to threaten the Albanians with abandonment, which allowed the KLA to exploit it. A US diplomat told Stephen Burg the following:

[The members of the negotiating team] knew the October agreement was a huge risk as the KVM [Kosovo Verification Mission] had no enforcement mechanism and the KLA was not party to it. I spent the next five months trying to persuade the KLA to honor something it did not sign or was consulted on. We all knew the agreement was shot full of holes. There was no alternative to open war, however. So we signed, took a deep breath, and did our best. (Burg, 2003, p. 82)

Some US officials, including Madeleine Albright, did issue stern warnings to the KLA. On one occasion Albright stated that the KLA had to behave "reasonably" or "they would lose completely the backing of the United States" (Albright, in Crawford, 2001, p. 514). The KLA decided, however, that this and other similar threats could be safely ignored. The confidence that the KLA had in the US commitment to intervene despite these threats and requests is very much in line with the moral-hazard logic. It is also undeniable that those Albanians who joined the KLA after Dayton and started criticizing Rugova's strategy had concluded that violence was more likely to attract the West's attention than pacifism, which is also something that the moral-hazard logic can comfortably claim as supporting evidence.

Ultimately, however, there are two major issues that are difficult to reconcile with the moral-hazard logic. First, the USA could in fact have made its threats of abandonment against Kosovo Albanians more credible. It simply chose not to. Or rather, it chose to do certain things that undermined the credibility of the few threats it did issue against the Kosovo Albanians. Not only could the USA have threatened abandonment credibly if it had wanted to, but it had the option of simultaneously coercing both the Serbs and the KLA, as will be explained below. Therefore, the claim that the USA was entrapped into supporting the KLA's radical agenda is not fully persuasive.[13] Second, even if the USA was entrapped by the KLA into protecting the Kosovo Albanians no matter what the KLA did, the US decision to present the Serbs with the ill-fated ultimatum at Rambouillet, which was the primary reason for the catastrophe that followed, does not follow logically. Let us deal with these claims in turn.

Why were the threats the USA made against the KLA ignored by the latter? The answer is very simple. Every time the USA made a statement condemning the KLA, the same statement contained a harsher condemnation of Serbs. Every time there was criticism of the KLA, the caveat that Serbs were the chief villains followed or preceded it. For example, Crawford quotes a statement by the US Special Envoy to the Balkans on 23 February 1998 that the KLA was "without any question a terrorist group" as evidence of a shift in policy from only deterring Serbs to trying to deter the KLA as well. Indeed, being branded a terrorist organization by the USA is a very serious charge, and in some circumstances might have had the intended chilling effect on the KLA. The problem is that there was something else in the statement missing from Crawford's quote. Here is the full statement:

The great majority of the violence we attribute to the [Serbian] police, but we are tremendously disturbed and also condemn very strongly the unacceptable violence done by terrorist groups in Kosovo, and particularly the UCK—the Kosovo Liberation Army. This is without any question a terrorist group. (Quoted in Burg, 2003, p. 76, emphasis added)

The USA actually decided to invite the KLA to become part of the political process *after* branding it a terrorist organization. This could hardly have escaped the KLA's attention. In fact, the worse the KLA behaved, the more intense the US contacts became with it (Burg, 2003, p. 78). The KLA, as a result, had few reasons to moderate its behaviour.

The tortured statements of US and NATO officials after the KLA single-handedly buried the Holbrooke Agreement are also good examples of the same problem. Here is an excerpt from a press conference by Ambassador William Walker:

I think we can look to both sides and say there have been instances of non-compliance on both sides. In our view the majority of the instances of non-compliance have emanated from the government side. But that is also perhaps a function of the fact that we have asked more of them. (Auerswald & Auerswald, 2000, p. 406)

In other words, the KLA broke the ceasefire and initiated hostilities, but both sides are equally responsible, perhaps the Serbs being slightly more responsible. According to an official in attendance, Ambassador Walker reported to a closed-door meeting of the North Atlantic Council that the "majority of the violations was caused by the KLA" (Walker, in Crawford, 2001, p. 514).

One of the explanations of this policy is provided by Crawford (2001), who argues that the USA could not have pressured the KLA too much, or withdrawn its support for the

Kosovo Albanians, without risking an emboldened Milosevic, who would interpret such a policy as a green light to unleash more violence in Kosovo. The USA was faced with a dilemma characteristic of situations he calls "pivotal deterrence" The third party, or the 'pivot', according to this argument, is often caught in a situation where it cannot force a change in the behaviour of one of the parties without simultaneously changing the behaviour of the other. More specifically, if it forces one of the parties to moderate its behaviour, it may inadvertently encourage the other party to become less moderate. This, Crawford argues, explains the US inability to get too tough with the KLA.

The dilemma Crawford describes is very real indeed, but its intensity is not constant. He himself argues in a more extensive study of this dilemma that its intensity depends on whether the conflicting parties being deterred have outside options (Crawford, 2003). The Kosovo Albanians had no such options. I would also argue that the dilemma is more manageable the more skewed the distribution of power is between the third party on one hand and the parties to the conflict on the other. The USA, in a word, was not in an impossible situation. It did have options.

The least attractive among the options was to give a green light to the Serbs to go after the KLA and issue a stern warning that any evidence of deliberate targeting of civilians would be severely punished. This may sound outrageous, but the USA routinely tolerates such and worse things elsewhere. Indeed, as already mentioned, the USA briefly allowed the Serbs to go after the KLA in summer 1998 with very positive results—i.e. a sidelined KLA, a strengthened LDK, which was willing to soften its insistence on outright independence, and also a Milosevic who was willing to make concessions after the successes against the KLA. The USA made a U-turn in September, but the point is that allowing the Serbs to fight the KLA was an option and it had been exercised with short-lived results that were in line with declared US preferences.

The second option was for the USA and NATO to inhibit the fighting themselves. As Crawford has pointed out, NATO could easily have blocked the arms supplies to the KLA by establishing control over a crucial ferry link from Albania (Crawford, 2001, p. 514). NATO could also have cut the supply of finances to the KLA, which would have had serious consequences for it. None of this was done.

There were also other much less controversial things the USA could have done, but did not. For example, it could have simply lent its strong backing to the negotiations between Rugova and Milosevic shortly after the arrival of the KLA on the scene in 1996. These negotiations had some early success, resulting in the so-called 'School Pact' on educational cooperation between the government in Belgrade and the Kosovo Albanians. They also held the promise of continued dialogue on other more difficult problems, but the process required strong third-party backing and guarantees. There was no interest in the West, however. The reason, according to Burg, is that many in the West feared that the success of this process would strengthen Milosevic (Burg, 2003, p. 73).[14] The aforementioned U-turn in summer 1998 may also have been the result of such fears.

All this, however, is less problematic for the moral-hazard argument than what transpired at Rambouillet and subsequently. This last chapter of the Kosovo drama is particularly difficult to reconcile with the moral-hazard theory. The Serbian attempt at ethnic cleansing in March–May 1999 was not retaliation against a KLA provocation, but against NATO's bombing campaign. And it is very difficult to argue that this campaign and the Rambouillet ultimatum, which was its precursor, were the result of entrapment. Indeed, some high ranking US officials, Madeleine Albright most prominently, saw the situation following Racak as an *opportunity* to bomb Serbia. Certain insiders told the media that Madeleine Albright was relentlessly advocating using force after Racak, because she realized that "the galvanizing force of the atrocity would not last long" (*New York Times*, 19 April 1999, p. 13). Notably this statement points in the exact opposite direction of the 'CNN effect'.

Ambassador Christopher Hill, who was one of the prominent American diplomats involved in the process, told the *Washington Post* that the US representatives knew that there was a 'zero point zero' chance that Serbs would agree to what they were offered at Rambouillet (*Washington Post*, 27 March 1999, p. A15). Another participant at Rambouillet told the press off the record that "we intentionally set the bar too high for the Serbs to comply" (quoted in Jatras, 2000, p. 24). This is also corroborated by a curious statement Albright made in an interview to the *New York Times*. According to her, Rambouillet was the key to "getting [the Europeans] to agree to the use of force" (*New York Times*, 18 April 1999, p. 13). Moral hazard, in short, seems to be a concept of questionable relevance for this most crucial part of the Kosovo tragedy.

An Alternative Rationalist Account of Third-Party Intervention and Escalation in Kosovo

If both the conventional wisdom and the moral-hazard account fall short of explaining the Serbian decision to escalate the conflict in Kosovo to a wholesale ethnic cleansing, what does? The starting point of the argument I will make here is the same as the starting point for the moral-hazard argument. Namely, I see state–minority disputes, including the ones involving violence, as bargaining problems, and not as cases of apolitical barbarism, which is frequently the assumption in the conventional wisdom. More often than not conflicts between states and minorities are political contests over divisible objects—power, status and territory. There are bargains in these disputes that both the state and the minority would prefer to violence, and more often than not *do* prefer to violence (Fearon & Laitin, 1996). Violence is costly for the state even in the most one-sided conflicts, even without the costs imposed by any third parties, and therefore it is inefficient *ex post*. Not all conflicts are resolved peacefully, of course. Violence against minorities, however, is usually a last resort used to coerce rather than simply hurt or destroy the minority, which is not unlike the role violence plays in conflicts between states (Fearon, 1995).[15]

State–minority conflicts are different from interstate conflicts in one crucial respect, nonetheless. While in interstate conflicts eliminating the opponent is rarely an option (Waltz, 1979, ch. 6; Goemans, 2000, pp. 31–34), in state–minority conflicts it often is. This does not mean that elimination is the preferred option by any means. Indeed, it is safe to assume that most states that have disputes with minorities see elimination as a solution that is too costly for a host of material and non-material reasons *ceteris paribus*. The state may prefer making concessions to, rather than eliminating, the minority. Moreover, if concessions do not work, coercive violence may seem a more attractive path than the wholesale elimination of the minority. The point, however, is that elimination is an option and that it is a qualitatively distinct alternative to violence that is 'merely' coercive.

What does all this have to do with intervention? I argue that interventions or threats of intervention often remove the coercive option for states and force them to choose between eliminating the minority or capitulating to its demands.[16] Even states otherwise reluctant to exercise such a radical option may do so if 1) intervention makes continued coercion either impossible or more costly than capitulation; 2) the state considers eliminating the minority less costly than capitulation; and 3) the state conjectures that the third party is unlikely to escalate the intervention to thwart the state's attempt to eliminate the minority.

This raises two additional questions. First, why would third parties force such a choice? Second, under what conditions is a target state likely to make the aforementioned conjecture? To answer the first question we need to distinguish between types of states based on the order of their preferences for eliminating the minority vs capitulating. It is conceivable, and not very rare empirically, that states faced with such a choice would rather concede than commit mass murder or ethnic cleansing. For example, after less repressive measures failed and the Soviet regime decided that it had to become much more draconian if it wanted to prevent its non-Russian republics from seceding, its repressive apparatus fortunately lost its nerve and decided to allow the dissolution of the country rather than use force massively. I will present evidence shortly that NATO decision makers, or at least the US decision makers, had decided that Milosevic was likely to cave in quickly rather than do what he ended up doing if presented with such a choice.

The answer to the second question is slightly more involved. One of the most common criticisms of third parties is that their threats to intervene often lack credibility. The conventional criticism is that such empty threats fail to make the situation better. But some scholars claim that such threats actually make things worse. Bloom (1999) has argued, for instance, that, although not credible, such threats unwittingly paint minorities into a 'fifth column' corner, making them a more likely target for elimination. Crawford focuses on a different mechanism, but also emphasizes the role of the insufficient credibility of NATO's threat in Kosovo. He writes:

> The combination of NATO's overwhelming power and underwhelming interest produced a predictable pattern of strategic interaction and moral hazard. NATO had to convince Serbia that it was as willing to fight as Serbs were, even though its motivation for doing so was much weaker. (Crawford, 2001, p. 504)

The problem with these and many other standard discussions of credibility of threats is that they set up the problem as a dichotomy: threats are either credible or not. Of course, if threats are not credible, then they cannot make anything worse, and if they are perfectly credible target states should surrender without a fight. But threats can be credible for certain things and not others, and for that reason we should avoid dichotomous definitions of credibility. Credibility should be seen as a continuum. In many cases third parties indeed are overwhelmingly more powerful but less resolved, as Crawford argues was the case with NATO's threat against Serbia. But this may mean the third party still has a credible ability to do things short of a full-scale war that can hurt the target-state. Issuing threats to do such things *can* be credible, and that is precisely the problem.

Sometimes, as in Kosovo, the problem is not just threats, but actual interventions. NATO's threat to intervene was carried out. Milosevic retaliated not against a threat, but against an actual intervention. What was at issue was not the credibility of NATO's threat to *intervene*, but the credibility of its threat to *escalate*, if Milosevic tried something more radical than coercion of Kosovo Albanians, which had been rendered impossible as a result of NATO's intervention.

But this brings us to yet another question. Was Milosevic's decision to raise the stakes by launching a campaign of mass expulsion rational? NATO eventually did see things through after all. Milosevic did have good reasons to be optimistic initially, however, based on several factors: the well articulated American and NATO reluctance to fight a ground war; Milosevic's calculation that NATO could not sustain its cohesion for too long; and the idea that turning the Albanians of Kosovo into refugees would provide him with bargaining leverage that his meagre military assets could not (Posen, 2000; Hosmer, 2001, pp. 22–43, Greenhill, 2003). The run-up to the war saw no build-up of NATO forces for a ground campaign, which made it abundantly clear that NATO's military action was going to be confined to air-strikes. There were internal and public discussions within the USA and among the NATO allies ruling out commitment of ground troops. Tony Blair told Bill Clinton in January 1999 that "ground troops could not be used to fight a war" (Daalder & O'Hanlon, 2000, p. 96). One hundred and ninety-one members of the US House of Representatives even voted against a resolution committing 4000 American peacekeepers to Kosovo *if both sides agreed to a peaceful settlement.* [17] The culmination of the process of inadvertently convincing Milosevic that he did not have to worry about a NATO ground invasion came on the same day that NATO launched the air-strikes. In his address to the nation on 24 March Bill Clinton declared that he "did not intend to put our troops in Kosovo to fight a war" (Clinton, 1999). In an interview with Jim Lehrer on the same day, Madeleine Albright similarly ruled out any deployment of ground troops. [18] In short, at the start of the bombing campaign Milosevic had good reasons to doubt the extent of NATO's commitment to escalate the war if he forced NATO's hand by expelling the Kosovo Albanians. [19]

I should mention that this US policy was not necessarily a result of shortsightedness, despite some criticisms to that effect (Daalder & O'Hanlon, 2000). The American leadership had to make sure it had both domestic and NATO support for its policy, and a ground war was a deal-breaker for both. [20] If the Clinton administration was set on intervening, it had no choice but to rule out the ground option publicly. The question then is whether the decision by the Clinton administration and NATO to intervene at all was rational. Couldn't they have predicted what Milosevic's reaction would be? One possible answer is that they simply did not care because the intervention had motives other than concern for the Kosovo Albanians. [21] While the actual motives were almost certainly not purely humanitarian, and while the criticisms of selective indignation and double standards are well deserved, it is not true, however, that NATO's leaders were unconcerned about the fate of the Kosovo Albanians. NATO's leaders did worry about Milosevic's reaction, but they concluded that he would surrender rather than unleash a campaign of ethnic cleansing. This is somewhat difficult to believe given the repeated public statements comparing Milosevic to Hitler and calling what was happening in Kosovo before the intervention genocide, but the record is clear. Here is what General Clark said in this regard:

> We thought the Serbs were preparing for a spring offensive that would target KLA strongholds, which had also been reinforced in previous months. *But we never expected the Serbs would push ahead with the wholesale deportation of the ethnic Albanian population.* (Clark, in Smith & Drozdiak, 1999, emphasis added)

Albright's policy planning staff had reached a similar conclusion in a study shortly before the war, where they tried to predict certain "unpleasant scenarios"

(*Washington Post*, 18 April 1999, p. A1). The CIA had conducted its own study trying to predict Milosevic's behaviour in response to the air-strikes. Its best guess was also a quick surrender by Milosevic after a few days of bombing (Sciolino & Bronner, 1999). This consensus was not affected even by Milosevic's explicit threat, made in a meeting with German Foreign Minister Joschka Fischer, to expel the Kosovo Albanians in response to an intervention.[22] Incidentally, as Kelly Greenhill observes, all of this is unequivocal evidence against the claim that the intervention was a response to an ongoing campaign of ethnic cleansing (Greenhill, 2003, p. 214).

Was it reasonable for the Americans to have made such an assumption given Milosevic's past? While it was a risky conclusion, and while the analysis that led to that conclusion had flaws,[23] it was not entirely unjustified. The reason is that Milosevic had earlier essentially abandoned the Krajina Serbs, had been the most cooperative member of the Balkan trio of himself, Tudjman and Izetbegovic at Dayton, and had also been cooperative on some occasions in Kosovo before Rambouillet. Moreover, American leaders were convinced that Milosevic was a weak-kneed, cowardly individual, who attacked the weak but would not stand up and fight if confronted by force. Peter Boyer cites a good example of this in a *New Yorker* article about Wesley Clark. Boyer writes that, in response to queries from Sandy Berger and General Joe Ralston, the Vice Chairman of the Joint Chiefs, who wanted to know what would happen if the bombing didn't work, Clark repeatedly answered: "I know Milosevic. It will work" (Boyer, 2003). This also was not an unreasonable belief, because on some past occasions Milosevic had become more cooperative when confronted with force. Even ignoring his threat to Joschka Fischer was not as outrageous as it seems, because he had incentives to misrepresent his true intentions in exactly that direction. He knew that Europeans were particularly afraid of having to deal with a flood of refugees (Greenhill, 2003, p. 214), and therefore he could have made the threat in an attempt to deter NATO without actually having the intention to expel the Kosovo Albanians.

Conclusion

The moral hazard theory of intervention is a welcome addition to a literature that sees violence against minorities as nothing more than a manifestation of misguided ideologies and murderous nationalism. The proponents of the theory are correct to point out that violence against minorities often results from political disputes rather than a simple preference for ethnic purity combined with an opportunity to kill. They are also correct to point out that the 'victim groups' often are strategic actors in their own right, and that their behaviour often contributes to violence. The central claim of the theory that the expectation of intervention may change the minority's bargaining calculus is also something that is difficult to disagree with.

Unfortunately, in its current form this theory has difficulty explaining certain puzzles. I have argued in particular that, while it can explain why minorities may behave recklessly and belligerently as a result of their expectations of intervention, the theory cannot adequately explain why eliminationist violence should be the outcome. For that we need an account of the target-state's bargaining calculus as well. We also need to explain why the minority and the third party fail to anticipate such escalation. I have also tried to demonstrate that, while moral hazard may have been *a* problem in Kosovo, it was not *the* problem. US policy did contribute to the KLA's belligerence and radicalism, but the explanation of the final outcome cannot be reduced to this fact alone. If the USA could take measures to mitigate the problem, but failed to do so, we need to ask why? Moreover, we need to explain why the USA failed to predict Milosevic's reaction to the intervention in March 1999, which was the direct cause of the catastrophic escalation that followed.[24]

What I have tried to do in this paper is to provide one such explanation. This attempt, however, is just that. There are still a number of unanswered and important questions, such as the question of why some optimistic minorities rebel and others do not. It is also not clear whether the explanations provided here can be generalized beyond Kosovo. More systematic testing will be necessary. What is clear, however, is that future research on third-party intervention should pay more careful attention to the incentives of the third parties and target-states in addition to the incentives of rebellious minorities, as well as to the question of how exactly these incentives interact.

Acknowledgements

An earlier version of this paper was presented at the annual conference of the American Political Science Association, Chicago, IL, September 2004. For their helpful comments I would like to thank Robert Jervis, Ron Hassner, Jack Snyder, R. Harrison Wagner and the participants of the Columbia University International Politics Seminar. I owe a special debt of gratitude to Alan Kuperman and Tim Crawford, who have been particularly generous with their time and wisdom. I would also like to acknowledge the support of the Olin Institute for Strategic Studies and the Belfer Center for Science and International Affairs at Harvard University, which made the research for this paper possible.

Notes

1. The argument in Jatras (2000) and Daalder and O'Hanlon (2000) is not that moral hazard was the principal cause of the conflict in Kosovo. Their studies do mention moral hazard as one of the problems, however.
2. For studies that dispute the existence of the 'CNN effect' as an independent cause, and argue instead that the 'CNN effect' is manufactured either by the government or the elites, see Herman and Chomsky (1988) and Carpenter (1995).
3. Cetinyan's argument assumes complete information, but the argument stands even if we assume incomplete information regarding the third party's preferences. In particular, if both the minority and the target-state are incompletely informed about the preferences of the third party, the assumption of rationality demands that their estimate of intervention be the same. For the general treatment of this claim for all interactions characterized by incomplete information, see Harsanyi (1967, pp. 163–166).
4. Ernest Gellner (1983) makes the observation regarding the relative rarity of demands for independence given the number of groups which could potentially press such demands. See also Fearon and Laitin (1996).
5. This evidence is presented in Burg and Shoup (1999, p. 113), and Kuperman (2003, p. 62).
6. On the problems associated with selecting on the dependent variable in general see Geddes (1990), and King *et al.*, (1994, pp. 129–137).
7. This is actually what happened in Kosovo as well, when the KLA arrived on the scene in 1996 and radically changed the situation without any visible shift in the behaviour of third parties.
8. Daalder and O'Hanlon (2000) make the most sophisticated case along these lines.
9. The most important problem in this account is the claim that NATO responded to an ongoing or planned mass expulsion. While the Serbian policy in Kosovo was indeed very repressive, and while there was quite a bit of violence in Kosovo before NATO's bombing campaign, there is little evidence that what the Serbs were doing was a systematic campaign of mass expulsion. The one potentially serious piece of evidence that, even if Serbs were not engaged in a campaign of systematic ethnic cleansing they planned to become so, was the so-called 'Operation Horseshoe', which was supposedly the blueprint for the operation of mass

expulsion of Kosovo Albanians that would have been put in motion even if NATO did not intervene. But the plan turned out to be a German forgery, as Human Rights Watch discovered. See Human Rights Watch (2001, p. 59). Moreover, operational plans do not necessarily reveal political intentions. Finally, I will present evidence later in the paper that NATO leaders not only did not think there was ongoing ethnic cleansing in Kosovo, they thought Milosevic was unlikely to embark on such a course even if painted into a corner.

10. Serbs were the most dispersed group in Yugoslavia, with large numbers of them living in Bosnia and Croatia, as well as other parts of the federation. For that reason Serbs were particularly sensitive to any weakening of the federation and had strongly discouraged all expressions of nationalism in Yugoslavia, including their own.

11. There was also a general rise of separatism in other parts of Yugoslavia, particularly in Slovenia and Croatia in the 1980s, which also contributed to the weakening of the Serbian commitment to 'Yugoslavism', and the rise of Serbian nationalism. For a detailed and excellent analysis of the causes of the rise of nationalism in Yugoslavia in the 1980s, see Woodward (1995, chs 2–4).

12. The KLA had held its first meeting in 1993, but it had no visible political presence in Kosovo until 1996.

13. Kuperman and Crawford have raised questions regarding the relevance of this issue in personal correspondence with the author. The relevant issue, according to them, is whether the the intervenor—the USA in this case—creates perverse incentives for risky behaviour by the minority—the Kosovo Albanians—regardless of whether the intervener could threaten abandonment or not. I disagree for two reasons. First, that claim is only correct if the object of analysis is the minority's behaviour rather than the outcome of an interaction between the intervenor and the minority. If we are trying to explain why conflicts between states and minorities escalate, however, rather than why minorities behave provocatively, the intervenor's choices are more than relevant. Second, the most basic puzzle underlying the moral hazard theory, and the reason we study it in this as well as other contexts, is why principals—third-party intervenors in this case—do things that produce outcomes that are less than optimal for them. The answer usually is some condition that either prevents the principal from observing the agent's—in this case the minority's—undesirable behaviour, or makes punishing the agent even costlier than absorbing the costs of the agent's undesirable behaviour, as I mentioned above. We cannot describe a problem as one of moral hazard if the principal knowingly and intentionally encourages reckless behaviour on the part of the agent.

14. The 'School pact' negotiations are interesting for another reason. It seems that Milosevic displayed a readiness to negotiate after his bargaining position against the Kosovo Albanians had improved considerably. More specifically, the 'School pact' negotiations took place after Dayton, where the West had refused to make a settlement in Kosovo a part of the comprehensive deal and had told the Kosovo Albanians that any settlement had to respect rump Yugoslava's territorial integrity (Vickers, 1998, pp. 286–294). This is definitely not sufficient to conclude that more NATO pressure on the Albanians would also have had a simultaneous moderating effect on Milosevic, but it is quite suggestive.

15. This rationalist account of violence between states is not universally shared either. But there is a tendency to see violence against minorities as fundamentally irrational even among those who do not see interstate wars as irrational.

16. I develop this argument formally and more extensively in Arman Grigorian, 'Third-party intervention and escalation of violence in state–minority disputes', PhD dissertation in progress, Columbia University. What follows is the more condensed and informal version.

17. The resolution passed with 219 votes in favour and 191 against, but the debates in the House left little doubt about the extent of the opposition to the intervention. The resolution also attached a large set of conditions to any deployment. It required, for instance, that the president report to Congress about what national interests were involved in Kosovo, what the costs were going to be, what the exit strategy was, etc. See Jessica Lee, 'GOP backs Clinton on Kosovo vote', *USA Today*, 12 March 1999, p. A1.

18. The interview is available on line at: http://www.pbs.org/newshour/bb/europe/jan-june99/albright_3-24.html.

19. In the end he gave up without a ground invasion. There was a gathering threat of ground invasion during the latter part of the air campaign, however, which in all likelihood strongly affected his decision to give up. Studies that make this claim include Daalder and O'Hanlon (2000), Byman and Waxman (2000) and Hosmer (2001). The best defence of the position that air power alone should be credited with victory is Stigler (2002/03). In any case, the threat of escalation to a ground war was not the only reason for Milosevic's decision to quit. The withdrawal of Russia's diplomatic support almost certainly played a major role as well. It should also be mentioned that the terms of his surrender were lighter than those of the Rambouillet ultimatum. On this, see Mandelbaum (1999) and Hosmer (2001, ch. 4).

20. Sandy Berger, who was Clinton's National Security Adviser, told Daalder and O'Hanlon that maintaining the fragile alliance and avoiding a congressional debate on the issue was why it was necessary to rule out a ground war and why Clinton had to make the aforementioned statement. See Daalder and O'Hanlon (2000, p. 97).
21. Such criticism has come both from the left and the right. See Chomsky (1999) and Carpenter (2000).
22. Milosevic stated that he could empty Kosovo in a week if there were an intervention. See Greenhill (2003, p. 214).
23. One such flaw was extrapolating from Milosevic's decision to go to Dayton and accept compromise there. The extrapolation was problematic because at Dayton Milosevic got carrots along with the sticks. Moreover, the air strikes that led to Dayton were accompanied by the Croatian conquest of Krajina. See Daalder and O'Hanlon (2000, p. 93). Some experts indeed predicted escalation before the fact. See Kuperman (1998a; 1998b).
24. One possible answer is incompetence, of course. Incompetence, however, is not an explanation, but a substitute for one.

References

Auerswald, P. E. & Auerswald, D. P. (Eds) (2000) *The Kosovo Conflict: A Diplomatic History Through Documents* (Cambridge, MA: Kluwer Law International).

Bloom, M. M. (1999) Failures of intervention: the unintended consequences of mixed messages and the exacerbation of ethnic conflict, PhD thesis, Columbia University.

Boyer, P. J. (2003) General Clark's battles, *The New Yorker*, 17 November.

Burg, S. L. (2003) Coercive diplomacy in the Balkans: the US use of force in Bosnia and Kosovo, in: R. J. Art & P. M. Cronin (Eds), *The United States and Coercive Diplomacy* (Washington, DC: United States Institute of Peace Press).

Burg, S. L. & Shoup, P. S. (1999) *The War in Bosnia–Herzegovina: Ethnic Conflict and International Intervention* (Armonk, NY: M. E. Sharpe).

Byman, D. L. & Waxman, M. C. (2000) Kosovo and the great air power debate, *International Security*, 24(4), pp. 5–38.

Carpenter, T. G. (1995) *The Captive Press: Foreign Policy Crisis and the First Amendment* (Washington, DC: CATO Institute).

Carpenter, T. G. (Ed.) (2000) *NATO's Empty Victory: A Post-Mortem on the Balkan War* (Washington, DC: CATO Institute).

Cetinyan, R. (2002) Ethnic bargaining in the shadow of third-party intervention, *International Organization*, 56(3), pp. 645–677.

Chomsky, N. (1999) *The New Military Humanism: Lessons from Kosovo* (Monroe, ME: Common Courage Press).

Clinton, B (1999) Address by the President to the Nation, White House, Office of the Press Secretary, 24 March 1999.

Crawford, T. W. (2001) Pivotal deterrence, and the Kosovo war: why the Hollbrooke Agreement failed, *Political Science Quarterly*, 116, pp. 499–523.

Crawford, T. W. (2003) *Pivotal Deterrence: Third-Party Statecraft and the Pursuit of Peace* (Ithaca, NY: Cornell University Press).

Daalder, I. & O'Hanlon, M. (2000) *Winning Ugly: NATO's War to Save Kosovo* (Washington, DC: Brookings Institution).

Dutta, P. K. (1999) *Strategies and Games: Theory and Practice* (Cambridge, MA: MIT Press).

Fearon, J. D. (1995) Rationalist explanations for war, *International Organization*, 49(3), pp. 379–414.

Fearon, J. D. & Laitin, D.D. (1996) Explaining interethnic cooperation, *American Political Science Review*, 90(4), pp. 715–735.

Geddes, B. (1990) How the cases you choose affect the answers you get: selection bias in comparative politics, *Political Analysis*, 2, pp. 131–152.

Gellner, E. (1983) *Nations and Nationalism* (Ithaca, NY: Cornell University Press).

Goemans, H. E. (2000) *War and Punishment: The Causes of War Termination, and the First World War* (Princeton, NJ: Princeton University Press).

Greenhill, K. M. (2003) The use of refugees as political and military weapons in the Kosovo conflict, in: R. G. C. Thomas (Ed.), *Yugoslavia Unraveled: Sovereignty, Self-Determination, Intervention*, pp. 205–242 (Lanham, MD: Lexington Books).

Harsanyi, J. (1967) Games with incomplete information played by Bayesian players, Part I, *Management Science*, 14(3), pp. 159–182.

Herman, E. & Chomsky, N. (1988) *Manufacturing Consent: The Political Economy of the Mass Media* (New York, NY: Pantheon Books).

Hosmer, S. P. (2001) *Why Milosevic Decided to Settle When He Did* (Santa Monica, CA: Rand Corporation).

Human Rights Watch (2001) *Under Orders: War Crimes in Kosovo* (New York: Human Rights Watch).

Jatras, J. G. (2000) NATO's myths and bogus justifications for intervention, in: T. G. Carpenter (Ed.), *NATO's Empty Victory: A Post-Mortem on the Balkan War* (Washington, DC: CATO Institute), pp. 21–29.

Judah, T. (2002) *Kosovo: War and Revenge* (New Haven, CT: Yale University Press).

King, G., Keohane, R. & Verba, S. (1994) *Designing Social Inquiry: Scientific Inference in Qualitative Research* (Princeton, NJ: Princeton University Press).

Kuperman, A. J. (1998a) NATO move may widen war, *USA Today*, 9–11 October.

Kuperman, A. J. (1998b) In Balkans: time to intervene?, *New York Times*, 5 October.

Kuperman, A. J (2002) Tragic challenges and the moral hazard of humanitarian intervention: how and why ethnic groups provoke genocidal retaliation, PhD thesis, MIT.

Kuperman, A. J. (2003) Transnational causes of genocide: how the West inadvertently exacerbates ethnic conflict, in: R. G. C. Thomas (Ed.), *Yugoslavia Unraveled: Sovereignty, Self-Determination, Intervention*, pp. 55–85 (Lanham, MD: Lexington Books).

Mandelbaum, M. (1999) A perfect failure: NATO's air war against Yugoslavia, *Foreign Affairs*, 78(5), pp. 2–8.

Posen, B. R. (2000) The war for Kosovo: Serbia's political–military strategy, *International Security*, 24(4), pp. 39–84.

Rowlands, D. & Carment, D. (1998) Moral hazard and conflict intervention, in: M. Wolfson (Ed.), *The Political Economy of War and Peace*, pp. 267–285 (Boston, MA: Kluwer).

Sciolino, E. & Bronner, E. (1999) How a president, distracted by scandal, entered Balkan war, *New York Times*, 18 April, p. 1.

Smith, R. J. & Drozdiak, W. (1999) Serbs' offensive was meticulously planned, *Washington Post*, 11 April, p. A1.

Stigler, A. L. (2002/03) A clear victory for air power: NATO's empty threat to invade Kosovo, *International Security*, 27(3), pp. 124–157.

Thomas, R. G. C. (2003) Sovereignty, self-determination, and secession: principles and practice, in: Thomas (Ed.), *Yugoslavia Unraveled: Sovereignty, Self-Determination, Intervention*, pp. 3–39 (Lanham, MD: Lexington Books).

Vickers, M. (1998) *Between Serb and Albanian: A History of Kosovo* (New York: Columbia University Press).

Waltz, K. N. (1979) *Theory of International Politics* (Reading, MA: Addison Wesley).

Weller, M. (1999) *The Crisis in Kosovo 1989–1999: International Documents and Analysis* (Cambridge: Documents and Analysis Publishing).

Woodward, S. (1995) *Balkan Tragedy: Chaos and Dissolution after the Cold War* (Washington, DC: Brookings Institution).

Conflict Management and the Misapplication of Moral Hazard Theory

ROBERT W. RAUCHHAUS

In recent years a small but growing number of scholars has examined third-party intervention and asked whether conflict management efforts can produce outcomes that are unexpected and unwanted (Bloom, 1999; Crawford, 2003; Terry, 2002; Kuperman, 2002; Rauchhaus, 2000). This question needed to be asked. The literature on humanitarian intervention and conflict management is often normatively driven and unduly influenced by wishful thinking. Scholars and practitioners often assume that intervention will either stop (or prevent) violence, or that it will fail to have any effect. Unfortunately, this is a false dichotomy. There is also a possibility that third parties can make matters worse.

Recent efforts to identify and explain some of the potentially adverse effects of humanitarian intervention have converged on the concept of moral hazard. Analysts have correctly identified several of the unintended consequences that may result from third-party intervention, but, as the following analysis suggests, these outcomes are generally not the result of a moral hazard. For a moral hazard to exist, a third party must be unable to observe the actions of an ethnic group or other domestic actor that is at risk. The key drivers of moral hazard are asymmetric information and hidden action.

This chapter evaluates the utility of moral hazard theory for the study of conflict management. The following section briefly reviews the scholarly literature on moral hazard. This step is necessary because it provides clear definitions and a good benchmark for evaluating efforts to apply moral hazard theory to conflict management. Section two builds a formal model of moral hazard where a third party must design a security guarantee that protects a group that is at risk from a hostile government. Section three evaluates the model and general utility of moral hazard theory. The final section discusses some of the steps that third parties can take to avoid moral hazard and points to issues that require further examination.

Moral Hazard and Conflict Management

The concept of moral hazard was first developed in the insurance industry. Moral hazards are manifest when insured parties engage in activities that increase their chance of being victimized by the risk against which they are insured. In other words, moral hazard refers to the tendency of people with insurance to change their behaviour in a way that increases claims against the insurance company.

Consider the case of car insurance. If an individual purchases an insurance policy, s/he may take fewer precautions than if s/he had no insurance. For example, car theft insurance may inadvertently encourage policy holders to park on the street rather than purchase off-street parking. Other examples of moral hazard abound. Federal deposit insurance might inadvertently encourage banks to make riskier loans; fire insurance might make policy holders willing to take greater risks, such as leaving the oven on while running errands; and, if a worker is laid off, unemployment insurance might decrease the urgency with which s/he seeks new employment.

Although concern for moral hazard has probably existed as long as there has been insurance, economists only began to carefully study the contracting difficulties associated with it during the past few decades. Pauly (1968) and contributors to a volume edited by Arrow (1970) initiated a fertile debate that shaped a decade of scholarship in economics on moral hazard. Zeckhauser (1970) represents one of the first efforts to model moral hazard formally. His study examined individual healthcare expenditures and the effects of proportional payment plans. Spence and Zeckhauser (1971) later offered a more general model of behaviour under uncertainty. Other studies offered explanations tailored to sharecropping (Cheung, 1969), capital markets and credit (Ross, 1973) and salary and pay structures (Stiglitz, 1974). Since the 1970s studies of moral hazard have proliferated in economics but the concept has received only limited attention in political science and international relations.

How might moral hazard theory be applied to the study of international relations and conflict management? Let us briefly consider a tailored version of the standard textbook example of insurance (Kreps, 1990, pp. 579–585; Mas-Colell *et al.*, 1995, pp. 478–488) such as coverage in the event of fire, and its analogy to humanitarian intervention. This is often referred to as the 'timeline' of moral hazard. First, the insurer (third party) will design a contract (security guarantee) and present it to the prospective client (ethnic minority or other group that is at risk). The contract may be written or oral and, regardless of whether it is detailed and explicit, or merely implicit, it must provide enough information that the insured might alter his or her behaviour.[1] Second, the prospective client must decide whether or not to purchase the policy. If the policy is too expensive given the coverage and likelihood of fire (war), the contract goes unsigned and the two parties do not enter into an agreement. If the policy meets the customer's needs and price point, then the policy is purchased and the parties enter into an agreement. Third, if the policy is accepted, the insured party will take actions during the contract period that affect the likelihood of fire (war). Unfortunately, these actions either cannot be directly observed by the insurer, or the monitoring costs are prohibitive (Kreps, 1990,

p. 581). The probability of a fire breaking out will depend on random events such as a spontaneous electrical box fire (or, analogously, an unprovoked government crackdown on a group) and the degree to which the insured party avoids risky behaviour (analogously, the group engaging in terrorism or other provocative behaviour). Finally, if there is no fire, the insured party receives no payment. But in the event of a fire, the insured party will receive a cash payment covering some of his or her damages (or humanitarian aid in the analogy).

When evaluating whether humanitarian intervention is producing a moral hazard, two issues require especially careful consideration. *For a moral hazard to exist, there must be a situation where the insuring party is not able perfectly to observe or monitor the insured party's behaviour.*[2] A key driver in moral hazard theory is asymmetric information. This is why economists use 'moral hazard theory' and 'theory of hidden action' interchangeably.[3] The third party cannot directly or perfectly observe the insured party's actions, but instead must infer them from the outcomes that result from both the insured party's actions and exogenous events. For a moral hazard to exist, the insuring party need not be physically unable to observe the insured party's behaviour. It may well be that, while the third party can theoretically observe the insured party's actions, s/he is unable to do so because monitoring is difficult or impossible because it is too costly or illegal (e.g. as a result of privacy laws).

In the case of moral hazard an insured party may become willing to take greater risks, but the goal is not intentionally to cause a bad outcome. *The concept of moral hazard, as generally discussed by economists, is distinct from fraud.* Key differences include the insured parties' motives, the legality of actions taken, and their preferences over outcomes. Good car insurance might inadvertently encourage speeding, but policy holders will not want to intentionally wreck their cars. Premiums, deductibles and the overall coverage value (e.g. vehicle replacement value) are purposefully designed in a way to eliminate an incentive to wreck a car. Moreover, in cases of fraud, there is also legal recourse or, at minimum, the contract may be voided. The concern for moral hazard does not primarily stem from the fact that some individuals may want to commit fraud, but rather that honest, rational, reasonable people might modify their behaviour in a way that exposes them to greater risk and increases claims against the insurance company.

Modelling Moral Hazard

In order to evaluate how well the moral hazard theory applies to the study of conflict management, let us formalize the approach with a simplified two-action, two-outcome model. Assume that a third party (insurer) is providing a security guarantee (contract) to a group that is at risk (insured party) which resides in a country where there is a dispute over regional autonomy. Assume that there are only two possible outcomes, either war or peace. The probability of peace, represented by π, is endogenous to the model and depends on the level of restraint of the group that is at risk and the random state of the world (θ). This is similar to moral hazard models that examine fire insurance where the probability of fire is a function of both the agent's actions and the chance that a short circuit or some other random event may cause a fire. To simplify matters, let us assume that the group that is at risk can only undertake one of two actions. The agent can either show a high level of restraint (H) or low restraint (L), which entails greater provocation. Both actions entail some cost, and $c_H > c_L$. If the group that is at risk shows a high level of restraint, then the probability of peace is π_H. The probability of war when exhibiting low levels of restraint is $1 - \pi_L$, where $\pi_H > \pi_L$.

The actors' utilities for the outcomes are as follows. For the group that is at risk the utility for the outcome of peace is represented by $u(p, c_i) = u(p) - c_i$, and the utility for war is $u(w, c_i, g) = u(w) - c_i + g$, where g represents the value of the benefits derived from the protection of the third party in the event of war. Assume that the domestic group is risk averse and that u is strictly concave. Consistent with moral hazard theory, the third party is unable to observe actions of the group that is at risk. Instead, the third party is only able to observe the outcome of war or peace. Assume that the third party is risk neutral, and utility for the peaceful outcome is represented by $t(p) = p$. The third party's utility for war is represented by $t(w,g) = t(w) - g$, where g is the cost of intervening in the dispute and providing some level of protection or bail-out to the group that is at risk.

Let us now sketch out the properties of a solution. When the potential exists for moral hazard, several conditions must be met for the third party and group that is at risk to have an incentive to enter into an agreement. First, the third party must make sure that the group that is at risk would rather accept the contract than pursue an outside option ($\underline{u}$), such as obtaining insurance coverage from a fourth party. This is known as the individual rationality constraint (IRC). If this first condition can be satisfied, the third party must next ask whether it is possible to create a security guarantee that creates an incentive for the group that is at risk to choose the action that the third party prefers. In other words, the third party must be sure that when the group that is at risk is addressing its own maximization problem, it will choose the third party's preferred level of restraint. This second condition is known as the incentive compatibility constraint (ICC).

Theoretically there is seldom a problem for a third party to determine an appropriate level of g and write a policy that encourages the group that is at risk to exercise the lower level of restraint. The third party must simply make the group that is at risk indifferent between this lower level of restraint (L) and the outside option ($\underline{u}$). Given that the insured party is assumed to be risk averse, it will prefer the guarantee over no guarantee. Moreover, when encouraging low levels of restraint, the insured party has no opportunity to cheat because there is no option below L.

In the case of conflict management we can limit our attention to cases where the third party is encouraging the group that is at risk to exhibit a high level of restraint (H). This is the more interesting case because it is here that moral hazard may exist: since the third party is unable to monitor the group's actions, it will intervene on behalf of the group in the event of war even if the group has caused the war by failing to exercise high restraint (and the group knows this). For the group that is at risk to prefer exercising a high degree of restraint (which entails higher costs but reduces the chance of war and intervention), we must first make sure that the ICC and IRC are satisfied. The ICC is met when the following conditions hold true:

$$\pi_H[u(p) - c_H] + (1 - \pi_H)[u(w) - c_H + g] \geq \pi_L[u(p) - c_L] + (1 - \pi_L)[u(w) - c_L + g]$$

The IRC is met when the expected value of either high or low restraint under the insurance policy is greater than the outside option. In this particular case we have defined the expected value of high restraint as larger, so the IRC is satisfied whenever:

$$\pi_H[u(p) - c_H] + (1 - \pi_H)[u(w) - c_H + g] > \underline{u}$$

We know that in equilibrium, the third party will craft an optimal contract (g^*) whereby the equations representing the ICC and IRC are equalities (see Appendix I for the solution for g^*). Given that the domestic group is risk averse, it will prefer to opt for this insurance rather than choose an outside option with the same or lower utility, so offering a level of g above the point of indifference would unnecessarily decrease the third party's payoff. Similarly, there is no reason to offer a level of g above the point that makes the group that is at risk indifferent between different levels of restraint. If both conditions are satisfied, then the ethnic group will prefer to exhibit greater restraint, which is more likely to produce a peaceful outcome. In order to determine whether an incentive exists for a third party to provide a security guarantee that encourages the group that is at risk to show a high degree of restraint, it is necessary to show that the third party's expected payoff for offering g_H^* is greater than the expected payoff for g_L^*.[4]

Goodness of Fit

How well does this model of moral hazard apply to the study of conflict management? To answer this question, it is helpful to work backwards from the outcome to the initial decision to offer a security guarantee. Given that a third party's first move will depend on an assessment of the last move, it is easier to treat this in a manner similar to backwards programming.

Preferences over Outcomes

Do the outcomes and players' preferences over outcomes reasonably portray the real world? Of course, instead of merely an outcome of war or peace, in reality there are intermediate range outcomes that may entail varying degrees of violence. The problem with the model, however, is not the simplifying assumption that there are only two outcomes, but rather the assumptions about the actors' preferences over outcomes.[5] Scholars concerned with the effects of moral hazard in conflict management often point to situations where the insurer prefers peace over war and the insured party prefers war over peace. For example, consider the case of Kosovo. Without the prospect of NATO intervention, attacks by ethnic Albanians on Serbian police and civilians could only lead to increased violence and a government crackdown. But if the government crackdown (war) triggers outside intervention (security guarantee), and if the outside intervention leads to *de facto* independence, then the outcome of war (and independence) is perhaps preferred to the outcome of peace (and limited regional autonomy). If an ethnic group prefers independence, and independence is only possible if there is war, then its preferences over outcomes are so completely misaligned with the third party that a contract should not have been offered in the first place.

For a third party logically to offer a security guarantee to an ethnic group that is at risk, the two parties must have similar *ex ante* preferences over outcomes. More specifically, the model suggests that when an ethnic minority prefers war to peace, the third party will generally lack an incentive to offer a security guarantee at reasonable values of g. This includes cases where the group strictly prefers war, $u(w) > u(p)$, and cases where the group prefers war if it brings intervention, $u(w) + g > u(p)$. Providing a security guarantee to an ethnic minority that strictly prefers war to peace does not make sense unless g has a negative value, and for g to have a negative value the third party must be able to sanction or punish the ethnic minority. This is unlikely because the conflict management cases examined by scholars generally entail third parties providing bail-outs ($g > 0$), not punishments ($g < 0$). In addition to the political difficulties of punishing an ethnic group, especially when things are already going poorly, a key assumption of moral hazard theory is that the third party cannot directly observe the ethnic minority's actions or identify bad behaviour. Thus one would have to punish the ethnic minority for the outcome of war without knowing who was responsible for it.

Crawford, Kuperman, and others are correct in pointing out that security guarantees sometimes create incentives for groups to show less restraint or even to prefer war. However, this will rarely result from moral hazard, which requires war to result in part from the group's unwillingness to pay the cost of restraint rather than from the group simply preferring war (with or without intervention) to peace. Instead, the unintended consequence is likely to stem from flawed contracts or uncertainty regarding the ethnic minority's preferences over outcomes.[6]

The Government's Actions

In a moral hazard analysis the government is essentially exogenous to the model. The primary issue under scrutiny is the relationship between the third party and the group that is at risk, not the interaction between the third party and the government, or the government and the domestic minority. This causes a number of problems. First, when one thinks of third-party intervention, the main interaction is usually between a third party and the government that is threatening to engage in a bloody crackdown. In the months leading up to Operation Allied Force, most of the interaction was between the US government and the Yugoslav government. Indeed, one of the main criticisms of the run-up to the war is that the USA failed to try to influence the KLA's behaviour. It seems odd therefore that a model would focus on the group that is at risk and largely ignore the government.

The failure to include the government as a strategic actor also raises a second question. If the group that is at risk is banking on intervention and views it as beneficial, why is the government not making good use of the same information? If the bargaining position of the group that is at risk has improved, this should lead the government to make greater concessions or avoid a crackdown that would trigger outside intervention. Thus it is unclear why humanitarian intervention would increase the probability of war. If one were to construct only a two-player model, the relationship between the third party and the government is perhaps the more important relationship to study. A three-player model would do even better.[7]

The Problem of Hidden Action

As mentioned above, moral hazard theory is also known as the 'theory of hidden action'. Here we find perhaps the most devastating critique of efforts to apply moral hazard theory to the study of humanitarian intervention and conflict management. If a third party has perfect information and is able to monitor the ethnic group's conduct and level of restraint, then coercive intervention *ipso facto* flunks the criterion for the existence of moral hazard.

Indeed, there is good reason to believe that moral hazard does not arise in cases of humanitarian intervention because third parties will either know, or with little or no cost could easily know, what type of actions are taken by groups that are at risk. The signs of provocation are not only in general easy to detect, they are often difficult to miss because the groups taking the actions are doing so precisely for the benefit of publicity. In the case of Kosovo, the *New York Times* and other media sources documented KLA bombings of police stations as well as hundreds of kidnappings, rapes and murders of Serbian civilians. While there were certainly multiple reasons for attacks, one of the main reasons was gaining domestic and international publicity.

There is another problem with the standard economics formulation of moral hazard theory as it applies to conflict-management efforts. In most economic models it is assumed that higher restraint is more costly for the group that is at risk, and that the third party's problem is crafting a contract that induces such higher restraint to increase the probability of the third party's preferred outcome. For this moral hazard model to apply, the costs (c_i) associated with higher levels of restraint (H) must be greater than the costs associated with lower levels of restraint (L). But for this assumption to make sense in the context of humanitarian intervention, one must assume that the costs to a group of showing greater restraint (e.g. loss of income or the psychological cost of sub-mission) are greater than the costs of engaging in violence or resisting the government. It is unclear when or under what circumstances this would hold true. One would normally expect that the KLA's strategy of less restraint (more violence) would be more costly than Rugova's strategy of high restraint (less violence).

Accepting or Rejecting a Security Guarantee

It is unclear whether a group that is at risk can meaningfully reject a security guarantee. The third party and government are often dyadicly interacting in a dispute, and even if the group that is at risk 'rejects' the terms of the security guarantee, the third party may nevertheless intervene if the crisis escalates to violence. Thus it is worth noting that an ethnic group's effort to reject the contract does not necessarily end the game, as it should in a moral hazard model.

Fire stations might provide a better analogy for humanitarian intervention than does fire insurance. The operation of fire stations by local government is in many ways structurally similar to humanitarian intervention because a homeowner does not have the option of opting out of coverage or protection. Moreover, it also removes or greatly reduces the problem of arson or fraud. Having a fire department nearby might reduce the risks associ-ated with lighting fireworks on 4 July but it will not create an incentive to burn down one's home. Fire departments try to put out fires, not rebuild houses or compensate owners for their losses. The main problem with this analogy is that the local governments have the authority and capability to compel property owners to pay taxes. Governments can also levy fines for unwanted or risky behaviour (e.g. not removing dead brush). As the next section suggests, it is far from clear whether third parties can extract much from an ethnic group that is at risk, although they clearly have some mechanisms for punishing bad behaviour.

Designing and Offering the Contract

With fire or car insurance the insured party pays a premium to the insurance company, and perhaps deductibles or co-payments in the event of claims. In the case of conflict management, however, it is unlikely that a group that is at risk will directly or indirectly make payment, monetary or otherwise, to a third party. The third party's 'payoff' is likely to come in the form of an improved international reputation, domestic political gains for preventing genocide abroad, or perhaps even 'savings' in the sense that early intervention might prevent a large-scale war.

The fact that payments do not flow from the insured party to the insuring party is significant, but this does not mean that the third party lacks instruments for manipulating premiums or deductibles. The third party can adopt a punishment strategy by condemning wrongdoing, withholding aid, applying economic sanctions or using force to stop unwanted conduct. But it should be noted that punishing a domestic group in another state is both difficult and costly. At the least, however, third parties should qualify their security guarantees with escape clauses and enough strategic ambiguity that, in the event that the domestic group is contributing to or causing the outbreak of hostilities (i.e. committing arson), the security guarantee is nullified.

Conclusion

Moral hazard occurs when there is an opportunity for agents to take 'hidden actions'. By contrast, in the realm of humanitarian intervention third parties are seldom unaware that their actions are emboldening some of the disputants. The concept of moral hazard is perhaps heuristically useful in that it helps to convey the presence of a perverse incentive structure, but scholars should not push the analogy too far. If the structural and informational attributes associated with humanitarian intervention are different from a moral hazard, then scholars might provide decision makers with irrelevant or even potentially harmful policy advice.

Instead of focusing on monitoring, future studies should focus on strategies to punish groups for actions that provoke government retaliation. Also in need of more treatment is the question of why third parties intervene in the first place if the failure or inability to punish bad behaviour will make matters worse. Some studies show that humanitarian intervention is helpful, while others suggest that it is harmful. This raises another question: under what conditions is humanitarian intervention most likely to succeed?

Although this analysis raises serious doubts about the general applicability of moral hazard theory to the study of humanitarian intervention, let us assume for the moment that it applies in some instances, which it undoubtedly does. How can third parties avoid creating moral hazard? The preceding analysis suggests five primary methods for reducing the likelihood that an insured party will engage in risky or otherwise undesirable behaviour. First, the third party can directly manipulate the payoffs associated with different outcomes in order to encourage the behaviour that is desired. Second, and separate from manipulating the benefits or costs associated with different outcomes (i.e. war or peace), the third party can devise punishments or create positive inducement for specific actions (i.e. provocation vs restraint). Third, the third party can improve monitoring capabilities in order to detect bad behaviour. Fourth, the third party can issue a security guarantee that includes escape clauses for fraud or arson. In some respects, this fourth option rests on the elements of previous options (detection and punishment), but it is identified separately because it leads to a state of the world where the contract is void. Finally, the third party can stay out of the conflict-management business and not offer a security guarantee in the first place.

Acknowledgements

For helpful comments, I thank Timothy Crawford, Benjamin Cohen, Peter Digeser, Garrett Glasgow, Alan Kuperman, Rose McDermott, Lorelei Moosbrugger, Christopher Parker Harrison Wagner and Barbara Walter. Kirk Lesh provided valuable research assistance.

Notes

1. An under-specified or ambiguous contract can cause problems if the insuring and insured parties have different views about the nature of the contract. Indeed, this may be one of the causes of unwanted outcomes in humanitarian intervention. Nevertheless, the security guarantee, by logical necessity, must be similar to a contract, otherwise the insured party's behaviour would not change. In international politics there is no external authority to enforce contracts; therefore contracts must be self-enforcing. In the case of humanitarian intervention costly signals, reputational effects and other costs might serve as a commitment mechanism that allows an insured party to realize that the insuring party is not merely engaging in 'cheap talk' that should be completely discounted.
2. Kreps defines moral hazards as situations "where one party to a transaction may undertake certain actions that (a) affect the other party's valuation of the transaction but that (b) the second party cannot monitor/enforce perfectly" (1990, p. 577). Using an example of a shop owner attempting to contract with a potential manager, Mas-Colell *et al.* (1995, p. 477) define moral hazard as "the inability to observe how hard [a] manager is working".
3. See, for example, Mas-Colell *et al.* (1995, p. 477) who discuss "the hidden action case, also known as moral hazard". Kreps (1990, p. 578) also uses the terms interchangeably, but notes that some scholars have attempted to make nuanced efforts to differentiate the two.
4. See Mas-Colell *et al.* (1995, pp. 487–488) for a discussion of these conditions.
5. Friedman (1966) and Waltz (1979) provide good explanations of why models and theories should be judged on their ability to explain or predict, not on whether their assumptions perfectly depict reality and can be deemed to be 'true' or 'false'.
6. On the problems associated with uncertainty over preferences before issuing a contract, see Rauchhaus (2005a) for a discussion of adverse selection.
7. For an analytic treatment of the three-player issue, see Crawford (2003). For a formal model of this issue, see Rauchhaus (2005b). Cetinyan (2002) also develops a three-player game where a third party intervenes, but the purpose of intervention is not conflict management. Instead, the third party is essentially a co-belligerent who supports the ethnic group.

References

Arrow, K. J. (1970) The economics of moral hazard: further comment, in: K.J. Arrow (Ed.), *Essays in the Theory of Risk Bearing* (Amsterdam: North Holland).
Bloom, M. (1999) Failures of intervention: the unintended consequences of mixed messages and the exacerbation of ethnic conflict, PhD thesis, Columbia University.
Cetinyan, R. (2002) Ethnic bargaining in the shadow of third-party intervention, *International Organization*, 56(3), pp. 645–677.
Cheung, S. N. (1969) *The Theory of Share Tenancy* (Chicago, IL: Chicago University Press).
Crawford, T. W. (2003) *Pivotal Deterrence: Third Party Statecraft and the Pursuit of Peace* (Ithaca, NY: Cornell University Press).
Friedman, M. (1966) The methodology of positive economics, in: M. Friedman (Ed.), *Essays in Positive Economics*, pp. 3–43 (Chicago, IL: University of Chicago Press).
Kreps, D. M. (1990) *A Course in Microeconomic Theory* (Princeton, NJ: Princeton University Press).
Kuperman, A. J. (2002) The moral hazard of humanitarian intervention, PhD thesis, Massachusetts Institute of Technology.
Mas-Colell, A., Whinston, M. D. & Green, J. R. (1995) *Microeconomic Theory* (New York: Oxford University Press).
Pauly, M. V. (1968) The economics of moral hazard: comment, *American Economic Review*, 58(3), pp. 531–537.

Rauchhaus, R. (2000) Third party intervention in militarized disputes: primum non nocere, PhD thesis, University of California, Berkeley.

Rauchhaus, R. (2005a) The principal–agent problem in third party intervention: moral hazard or adverse selection?, paper presented at the IGCC Junior Faculty Colloquium, San Diego, CA.

Rauchhaus, R. (2005b) Third parties, coercive intervention and conflict management: a game theoretic approach, paper presented at the 2005 Annual Meeting of the American Political Science Association, Washington, DC.

Ross, S. (1973) The economic theory of agency: the insurer's problem, *American Economic Review*, 63(2), pp. 134–139.

Spence, M. & Zeckhauser, R. (1971) Insurance, information, and individual action, *American Economic Review*, 61(2), pp. 380–387.

Stiglitz, J. E. (1974) Alternative theories of wage determination and unemployment in LDCs: The labor turnover model, *Quarterly Journal of Economics*, 88(2), pp. 194–227.

Terry, F. (2002) *Condemned To Repeat? The Paradox of Humanitarian Action* (Ithaca, NY: Cornell University Press).

Waltz, K. N. (1979) *Theory of International Politics* (Reading, MA: Addison-Wesley).

Zeckhauser, R. (1970) Medical insurance: a case study of the tradeoff between risk spreading and appropriate incentives, *Journal of Economic Theory*, 2(1), pp. 10–26.

Appendix I

To solve the model, allow the ICC and IRC to hold with equality, and then combine the two equations to yield the following:

$$\underline{u} = \pi_L[u(p) - c_L] + (1 - \pi_L)[u(w) - c_L + g]$$
$$\underline{u} = \pi_L u(p) - \pi_L c_L + u(w) - c_L - \pi_L u(w) + \pi_L c_L + (1 - \pi_L)g$$
$$\underline{u} = \pi_L u(p) + u(w) - c_L - \pi_L u(w) + (1 - \pi_L)g$$
$$\underline{u} = \pi_L[u(p) - u(w)] - c_L + u(w) + (1 - \pi_L)g$$
$$g^* = [\underline{u} - \pi_L[u(p) - u(w)] + c_L - u(w)]/(1 - \pi_L)$$

For a discussion of less restricted models (e.g. multi-effort, multi-outcome), see Mas-Colell *et al.*, (1995).

Illusions of Moral Hazard: A Conceptual and Empirical Critique

JON WESTERN

The logic of unintended consequences and perverse incentives is not new to international relations theory. For example, critics of collective security have long argued that such arrangements are inherently weak because they lead to free-riding, insufficient balancing and, in some rarer instances, more aggressive and provocative diplomacy among its members who are less fearful of retaliatory response (Betts, 1992; Kupchan & Kupchan, 1991; Mearsheimer, 1994). Ultimately many conclude that, despite the good intentions of those advocating collective security, the unintended result is a world made less safe.

It is thus not surprising to see the emergence of a literature that critically examines the potential unintended consequences associated with the rise of norms of humanitarian intervention. The theory of moral hazard and humanitarian intervention, however, raises some very provocative and unsettling claims: that the rise of international norms of humanitarian intervention has made matters worse by creating perverse incentives that encourage rebel groups to provoke genocidal retaliation by state authorities, in the expectation that such violence will compel international intervention on their behalf. In other words, not only do norms of humanitarian intervention lead to more war, they can and do lead to genocide. At face value the theory seems to have an intuitive and deductive logic—established practices of international intervention provide an expectation of additional resources to aggrieved groups who are not otherwise able to challenge and overthrow state authorities. The expectation arises from the emergence of norms of humanitarian intervention that are triggered in response to high levels of violence against civilian populations.

However, a closer examination of the logic, the concepts and the empirical record reveals deep flaws with both the theory and the empirical findings and conclusions. In short, there is little or no evidence that norms of humanitarian intervention have made matters worse. In fact, as I present in the conclusion of this chapter, there is some evidence to suggest that these emerging norms have achieved what they set out to do— they have saved lives and they have contributed in part to the reduction of ethnic and civil conflicts in the past decade.

In this chapter I argue that the theory of moral hazard and international intervention is problematic on several grounds. First, the argument rests on the weak empirical premise that most victims of genocide or politicide are 'responsible for initially militarizing' conflicts and 'provoking' genocidal retaliation. Second, its claim that such seemingly suicidal rebellion is the result of perverse incentives created by emerging norms of humanitarian intervention is largely *post hoc* and rests on poorly specified and under-conceptualized variables. The result is a model that has yet to establish any testable or falsifiable propositions. Finally, the overall argument does not square with broader empirical findings that reveal a significant reduction in the number and frequency of civil and ethnic conflicts during the timeframe when the norms of humanitarian intervention have emerged.

My intent in this chapter is not to provide an exhaustive alternative explanation for the empirical cases presented in the earlier chapters that are used to illustrate the theoretical elements of moral hazard. Rather, I intend to present a methodological and empirical critique of the theory of moral hazard as applied to the issue of humanitarian intervention. I do not discount that some rebel groups are responsible for participating in and triggering violence, although I believe the impression left by the other chapters that this is a common or robust empirical finding is wrong. I also do not dismiss the claim that rebel groups seek outside intervention. If one assumes they are rational actors, they most certainly would seek external assistance, and every case of state-sponsored violence against any religious, ethnic or racial minority almost always generate appeals for international assistance. For that matter, almost all cases of interstate war exhibit the same appeals—the UK, for example, engaged in extensive propaganda efforts and appeals, citing German atrocities, in the hopes of soliciting US entry into both World War I and World War II (Lavine & Wechsler, 1940). But the fact that there are efforts to secure international aid and intervention does not establish causality. Ultimately the literature on civil and ethnic violence reveals that the motivations for and causes of violence are far more complex than a simple linear causal flow from international norms to provocation to genocide.

Provocation: No Evidence, No Puzzle

The theory of moral hazard as applied to international intervention suggests that leaders of groups provoke genocidal and politicidal retaliation against the groups they claim to represent. Establishing support for this empirical claim is important because the theory rests on the logic of perverse incentives—international norms cause victim groups to engage in risky and provocative behaviour to lure international assistance to their cause. In the moral hazard argument presented in this volume this provocative behaviour is both an intervening and a dependent variable. It is the intervening variable leading to genocidal retaliation by state authorities, but it is the dependent variable presented as an empirically puzzling phenomenon that needs explanation: why rebel groups take the seemingly irrational action of intentionally provoking genocidal retaliation.

But is there really a pattern of such suicidal rebellions and has it been established? Do most victim groups provoke the violence against themselves? The short answer is no. Alan Kuperman states that there is a "surprising" empirical puzzle in that "most ethnic groups that fall victim to genocidal violence are responsible for initially militarizing the conflict" (Kuperman, 2006, p. 2). He also states that the evidence of this is "robust", which he bases on an analysis of data collected by Barbara Harff and Ted Robert Gurr, who compiled data on 44 cases of genocide and politicide from 1945 to 1988 (Harff & Gurr, 1988). In reviewing these data Kuperman concludes that 30 of the 44 cases of politicide were the result of the victim group provoking "their own group's demise by *violently challenging* the state's authority" (Kuperman, 2006, p. 3, emphasis added). Harff and Gurr, however, make no such representation of the presence of a violent challenge. For example, they describe 15 cases of repressive politicides as instances in which the ruling groups retaliated against "adherents of political parties, factions, or movements because of their support for oppositional activity" (Harff & Gurr, 1988, p. 368). Moreover, their list of repressive politicides includes two types of cases: those perpetrated by military regimes, for example in Guatemala, El Salvador, Chile and Argentina, to execute and eliminate communist or leftist sympathizers; and cases that involved aggressive violence perpetrated by the likes of Idi Amin in Uganda, Mobutu Sese Seko in Zaire, and Francisco Macias Nguema in Equatorial Guinea. Here the new leaders used, according to Harff and Gurr, "extreme and deadly repression against any and all groups *suspected of opposition*" (Harff & Gurr, 1988, p. 369, emphasis added).

Contrary to Kuperman's interpretation that these cases represent victim groups initiating "violent challenges" against the state authority, several of the cases, such as Argentina, Chile, El Salvador, Equatorial Guinea, Indonesia, Pakistan (Baluchi tribesmen), Uganda, the USSR and Zaire all have well documented literature concluding that violence was initiated by state authorities to suppress political opposition emerging in response to concerns over resource allocation, property rights, development strategies, repression, and political participation (Khan, 2003; Wickham-Crowley, 1992). In some of these instances, violent insurgencies grew out of the initial state-sponsored violence; in other instances, however, such as Argentina, Chile and Equatorial Guinea, no formal insurgency emerged.

Who's Provoking Whom?

Even if one were to concede that some of the cases exhibit active and violent action by rebel groups, such violence often does not occur in a vacuum outside significant repression or coercion. Ultimata, protracted periods of police brutality, curfews and other forms of crack-down, expropriation of property or forced migration may all precipitate armed rebellions. In the two cases most frequently examined in the literature on moral hazard theory and humanitarian intervention—Bosnia and Kosovo—the militarization of the conflict and the run-up to war demonstrate a much longer timeframe that included escalating reciprocal political repression, protest and violence that seem much more consistent with alternative explanations for the causes of war than the simple linear trajectory offered by moral hazard.

Bosnia. Kuperman makes several strong assertions characterizing the outbreak of war in Bosnia. He states that the Muslims "organized and armed a 100 000-strong militia and (with the republic's Croats) declared Bosnia's independence in March 1992, against the will of Belgrade and the republic's Serbs, knowing this would trigger war and genocidal violence" (Kuperman, 2006, p. 10). He later states that "Bosnia demonstrates that some armed challenges are launched by groups who face no discrimination" (Kuperman, 2006, p. 17).

The argument that Bosnia fits the logic of suicidal rebellion is problematic on several fronts. The war in Bosnia and the secessionist moves by Bosnian Muslims and Croats occurred within the broader context of a long history of ethnic and political rivalries, the dramatic rise and manipulation of nationalism in the late 1980s and early 1990s, the disintegration of centralized state institutions in the federation that began in the late 1980s, and fierce fighting in neighbouring Slovenia and Croatia in the run-up to the war in Bosnia. In short, the causes of the secessionist moves in Bosnia or the war there cannot be treated in isolation from powerful indigenous political, economic and social factors associated with the disintegration of the Yugoslav federation.

An example of this is Kuperman's statement that the Bosnian Muslims faced no discrimination. This ignores the complex and virulent political and nationalist processes unfolding from 1989 to 1992. Serbian leader Slobodan Milosevic's rise to power, with his blatant appeals to Serb nationalism and his decision in 1989 to usurp the 1974 constitution granting autonomy to Kosovo and Vojvodina, triggered the rapid disintegration of the Yugoslav federation. Milosevic's efforts to re-centralize economic and political control in Belgrade clashed with the ideas of political and economic decentralization in Slovenia and Croatia and the broader liberalization process spreading throughout all of Eastern Europe in late 1989 and 1990. This fight over the future direction of power and authority in the federation fuelled not only the rise of Serb nationalism, but intense nationalist sentiments in Croatia, Slovenia and Bosnia as well. The rise of Serb nationalism and Milosevic's crackdowns against Muslims in Kosovo and the Sandzak region of Serbia fuelled intense anxiety among Bosnia's Muslim population.

Well in advance of the events of the independence referendum in Bosnia in early 1992 and of any possible expectation of international intervention, the political positioning of the nationalist leaders and their parties was put in motion. In September 1990—18 months before the war in Bosnia—Bosnian Muslim leader Alija Izetbegovic announced that, if Croatia and Slovenia withdrew from the federation, Bosnia would seek independence and would not stay in a Serb-dominated rump Yugoslavia (Burg & Shoup, 2000, p. 47). This reflected a deep-seated view among Bosnian Muslim nationalists that their status would be greatly diminished under Serb-dominated rule. Indeed, the success of the three nationalist parties in Bosnia in the November 1990 parliamentary elections reflected deep anxiety and fear of discrimination among the population. It also led to a wave of repression and discrimination in community after community throughout the republic.

Moreover, the question for many in Croatia and Serbia in 1991 and 1992 was not Bosnian independence, but Bosnian partition to form a Greater Croatia and Greater Serbia.

Croatian President Franjo Tudjman and Serbian President Slobodan Milosevic, as well as Bosnian Croat leader Mate Boban and Bosnian Serb leader Radovan Karadzic, met several times between 1990 and 1992 to discuss partition of Bosnia (Woodward, 1995, pp. 172, 216). During 1991 the nationalist leaders of all three groups were escalating their rhetoric and policies of exclusion and discrimination throughout Bosnia. The most vulnerable of the three in this process were the Bosnian Muslims.

Furthermore, there is little evidence that it was the Bosnian Muslim leadership that *initially militarized* the conflict. It is fair to say that, even before the end of the war in Croatia, the Bosnian Muslims, Croats and Serbs all began preparing for war in Bosnia. The Serb-dominated Yugoslav National Army was well entrenched there (several units had been redeployed there after the outbreak of violence in Croatia) and Serb paramilitary units moved into Serb areas of Bosnia in 1991 and began distributing weapons (Silber & Little, 1997, pp. 216–221). The Croats relied heavily on weapons transfers from Croatia. Furthermore, many Serbs and Croats living in Bosnia had fought against one another in the war in Croatia and returned home with their weapons and units intact. In fact, fighting and skirmishes between Serbs and Croats in Bosnia began in Mostar in autumn 1991 and in Bosanski Brod in early 1992. For their part the Bosnian Muslims assembled a militia, but this process developed much more slowly than in Serb and Croat areas (Woodward, 1995, pp. 250–264).

Nor is there significant evidence that the Bosnian Muslims 'knew' or expected that their actions would trigger war and genocidal violence and that this was the basis of their calculations in the run-up to the war in 1992. On the contrary, the evidence points to a number of missed opportunities, miscalculations and misguided political decisions by all groups to reject compromise as the main elements leading to the war (Gagnon, 2004; Burg & Shoup, 2000; Woodward, 1995; Zimmermann, 1999). Indeed, as Susan Woodward concludes, what is striking about the Bosnian Muslims and their leadership is that amid all of rumours and preparations for fighting, "all of Sarajevo was convinced that it would be spared war" (Woodward, 1995, p. 18).

The failings and missteps of the international community are also well documented (Gow 1997; Moore, 1992; Woodward, 1995). The principal findings in this literature are that the international community failed to prevent or deter the outbreak of war. But the primary motivations for war came from within Yugoslavia. The preponderance of the scholarship on the causes of war in Bosnia points to the significant influence of complex internal political and structural processes. These included the disintegration of government authority and the intersection of politically mobilized nationalist and ethnic rivalries. The rivalries gained salience through the emergence of weak leaders with no experience or desire for compromise, as they engaged in competition to capture the residual economic and political resources up for grabs in the transition, eventually leading to war.

Kosovo.   The second case study frequently cited to support the theory of the moral hazard of humanitarian intervention is Kosovo. While this case does present stronger evidence of violence attributed to the KLA, it is still problematic on the question of who provoked whom. For example, both Crawford and Kuperman begin their assessment of the initial militarization of the conflict with the events of 1998. The selection of 1998 is largely *post hoc* and overlooks a much deeper trajectory into violence. As established in the chapter by Arman Grigorian, the origins of the KLA and its response to Serb repression were long in the making (Grigorian, 2006). A full 30 years before October 1998 Kosovo Albanians pressed for greater autonomy from Serbia within the Yugoslav federation. Episodes of repression, demonstrations and reprisals occurred throughout the 1970s, 1980s and 1990s. In 1981, as many as 300 Kosovo Albanians were killed when the government moved in to crack down on Kosovo-wide demonstrations that began at the University of Pristina (Amnesty International, 1985, p. 12).

As noted, Slobodan Milosevic's unilateral 1989 usurping of the constitutional status of Kosovo and Vojvodina and the subsequent power shift this created in the federal presidency contributed to widespread fears and concerns not only in Kosovo but throughout Slovenia, Croatia and Bosnia. This was a major development in the disintegration of the Yugoslav federation. By revoking the autonomous status of Kosovo and Vojvodina, Milosevic gained effective control of five votes on the nine-member collective presidency (Serbia, Montenegro, Vojvodina, Kosovo and the Yugoslav Federal Army Chief of Staff). This step—coupled with Milosevic's clear designs to recentralize control over the federal political and economic institutions and his blatant appeals to incite Serb nationalist sentiment in Kosovo, Krajina, eastern Slavonia and elsewhere throughout the federation—were clearly the precipitating causes fuelling the secessionist movements in Croatia, Slovenia and Bosnia.

Crawford argues that the emergence of the KLA occurred following the political crisis in neighbouring Albania in spring 1997 that allowed weapons to be transferred into Kosovo (Crawford, 2006). The KLA 'provocation', however, comes a full eight years after the Serbs revoked Kosovo's autonomous status. Throughout the 1990s human rights organizations and the US State Department Human Rights reports identified consistent widespread and systematic Serb abuses in Kosovo (Mertus, 1998). Furthermore, in 1995, Belgrade initiated a policy to resettle Serbs displaced from Croatia in Kosovo.

The refusal by the international community to allow Kosovo Albanian participation at the Dayton negotiations to end the Bosnia war in November 1995 created significant fissures among Kosovo Albanians. Most significantly the failure to gain a seat at the table at Dayton fuelled a challenge to Kosovo's pacifist leader Ibrahim Rugova by the Kosovo Liberation Army (KLA), which believed in the need for violence and self-defence against Serb repression. Amid repression by Serbs in Kosovo, the KLA surfaced in 1996 claiming responsibility for a series of bombings against Serbs. Rumours that Serb paramilitary leader Arkan had been deployed to Kosovo in late 1997 suggested that Belgrade was going to ratchet up its pressure on all dissent, because Arkan had deployed to Bosnia before the outbreak of war there and his forces launched some of the earliest and most violent attacks against Bosnian Muslim civilians (Burg & Shoup, 2000, p. 119; Zimmerman, 1999, p. 195). In Kosovo's environment of rising repression the KLA launched an increasing number of attacks on Serb authorities and civilians.

The question of who provoked whom is an important part of the story for moral hazard logic. The theory of moral hazard relies on clarity of the intervening variable—that rebel groups initiated violence (because they were confident they could expect intervention). However, both Bosnia and Kosovo reveal an on-going and gradual escalation of political contestation, repression and opposition, and ultimately violence. This longer trajectory is important because it expands consideration of the strategic context, and ultimately the motivations, under which victim groups act.

Negative Precedents and Perverse Incentives

The second element of the argument of moral hazard theory is that the alleged risky behaviour is the result of perverse incentives and negative precedents created either by explicit pledges of international intervention or simply by the emergence of new norms of humanitarian intervention. Ultimately, as this section discusses, the advocates of moral hazard theory have not sufficiently specified the concepts of perverse incentives, negative precedents and international norms.

Kuperman develops his argument by laying out an empirical puzzle—the phenomenon of suicidal rebellions—and then discusses the inability of existing arguments to explain rebellion and violent resistance. He then uses the weakness of the existing literature to introduce his theory of the perverse incentives associated with emerging norms of humanitarian intervention as a stronger explanation. But, even if one were to accept Kuperman's argument on the existence of suicidal rebellions, it is curious that the evidence used to establish the phenomenon predates the existence of the explanatory variable: the emergence of norms of humanitarian intervention. Harff and Gurr (1988) present cases from 1945–87. Not only was there no norm of intervention, and hence no expectation of intervention by the victim group, Harff and Gurr explicitly justify their decision to exclude cases from before 1945 because they wanted "to focus attention on the frequency of such deadly episodes since the world community became aware of the atrocities committed during the Holocaust . . . yet seemingly did nothing to prevent recurrence of similar events on a lesser scale" (1988, p. 362). In other words, not only did no norm of intervention exist, there was a very robust pattern of lack of humanitarian intervention at the very time of alleged wide-spread suicidal rebellions. Something other than the expectation of intervention must be driving the phenomenon.

The Role of Norms and Precedents

More broadly, however, there is the deeper problem of conceptualizing the role of international norms and precedents in international politics. To take just one example, Crawford argues that a cause of perverse incentives is negative precedent which he defines as "an example that is followed or copied" (Crawford, 2006, p. 27). Using this definition, a precedent can only be established by repeated action. Yet Crawford illustrates the concept of negative precedent by citing Paul Schroeder's criticism of the Bush Doctrine—a criticism that Crawford suggests is motivated by the concern that it "set a dangerous and negative precedent which will lead other countries to launch pre-emptive wars" (Crawford, 2006, p. 28). By this definition it will only become a precedent when it is sufficiently copied or followed. It may become a precedent but clearly it is not one yet. Later, Crawford makes reference to President George H. W. Bush's decision to launch Operation Provide Comfort to aid the Kurds in northern Iraq in April 1991. Crawford describes it as the creation of "precedent-setting humanitarian safe-zones . . . which would raise expectations for such intervention throughout the decade" (Crawford, 2006, p. 36).

Similarly, Kuperman invokes the term 'emerging norms of humanitarian intervention' as the critical variable. The problem with attributing causation to the role of 'emerging norms', is that of *a priori* specification. At their core norms are collective expectations of appropriate action. They are generated over time through the repeated invocation of appropriateness and ultimately some semblance of compliance. While the process of norm generation is still the source of much scholarly attention and debate, one consensus does seem to exist: they are difficult and slow to develop. Writing in 1996 Martha Finnemore concluded that the norms of intervention had created a permissive condition for humanitarian intervention, but that they do "not ensure behavior" (Finnemore, 1996, p. 158). Writing later, in 2003, Finnemore concluded that it was the events of the 1990s, including the interventions in Somalia, Bosnia and Kosovo, and the non-intervention in Rwanda, that provided the collective international experiences that strengthened the norms of humanitarian intervention (Finnemore, 2003, pp. 78–79).

Elizabeth Kier and Jonathan Mercer also argue that precedents—either positive or negative—are very difficult to establish (Kier & Mercer, 1996). They identified three principal elements in the process of establishing precedent for action. First, there must be a common interpretation about the act (i.e. a humanitarian intervention must be seen as a humanitarian intervention and not as an intervention motivated purely by self-interest). Second, there must be followers—others must use the precedent to order their expectations or to shape their behaviour. Third, a precedent must be conspicuous—you know the conditions under which the precedent is to be invoked.

Bosnia.   In their analysis of the war in Bosnia, Kier and Mercer found that neither military intervention nor non-intervention were likely to set a precedent because, first, the international community disagreed widely on the nature and purpose of military intervention and the use of force in general. Second, they argued that the case of Bosnia revealed only the latest example of widespread reluctance on behalf of the international community to intervene even amid "unspeakable human rights violations". And third, they argued that, throughout the debates on Bosnia, the nature of the conflict was ambiguous and the norm of intervention came into conflict with the norms of sovereignty, so no clearcut consensus emerged on when intervention would be appropriate. Ultimately, Kier and Mercer concluded that "conditions necessary to set a precedent are demanding and rarely met. Because precedents are social constructions, we cannot easily manipulate them to suit our interests" (Kier & Mercer, 1996, p. 99).

To the extent that a norm of international humanitarian intervention has evolved, it appears to result from the interventions of the 1990s. This makes the use of norms as an explanation for Bosnia more problematic, because the outbreak of war there in 1992 predates the interventions in Somalia, Haiti, Bosnia in 1995, Kosovo, Sierra Leone and Haiti again. It is difficult to argue for the causal influence of norms before they existed with any significant strength.

Furthermore, arguments that posit the influence of norms and precedents must account for the multiple and mixed signals coming from the international community. In the case of Bosnia for example, not only was there no evidence of a robust norm of intervention, the strong signal consistently delivered by the international community—in both its words and its actions—was that it was very reluctant to intervene in regional and civil violence. In January 1992, at the time Kuperman claims the Bosnian Muslims were ratcheting up their provocations against the Serbs because they expected international intervention if the Serbs retaliated, the International Committee of the Red Cross warned that Somalia was the world's worst humanitarian tragedy, that 300 000 civilians were already dead, and that two-thirds of the country's six million inhabitants were at risk of death by starvation. Despite Somalia's grave humanitarian situation and increasing violence, the UN withdrew its entire relief staff in autumn 1991, and the USA and Europe all but ignored the pleas for aid for an entire year as the situation deteriorated.

In addition, although the USA had deployed troops to northern Iraq as part of Operation Provide Comfort in April 1991, throughout the operation US military commanders and political leaders repeatedly emphasized that the action was an isolated event and not a precursor of things to come (Tyler, 1991). More importantly, Operation Provide Comfort was a very limited humanitarian mission to feed and care for Kurdish refugees who had been forcibly displaced by Saddam Hussein. The USA encouraged both the Kurds and the Shiite majority in Iraq to rise up and overthrow Saddam Hussein after the Persian Gulf war. After Saddam responded with brutal suppression of both groups, the Bush administration and the international community responded with only a limited humanitarian mission in the north and the establishment of a no-fly zone in northern and southern Iraq. Neither the Bush administration nor the international community did anything to assist either group to advance its political aspirations significantly.

Furthermore, in the case of Yugoslavia at least, at each stage in the run-up to the wars in Croatia and Bosnia the categorical language from the USA and the international community was that it was not going to intervene. James Baker's casual disclaimer that "We don't have a dog in that fight" was the well known position of the US government and also reflected the view of most European capitals. During the critical period from early 1990 to June 1991, the USA did not hold any high-level talks with senior Yugoslav officials (in fact, in 1990 Yugoslav Prime Minister Ante Markevic was discouraged from visiting Washington for discussions) and US officials largely refused any direct contact with the rising nationalists leaders throughout the federation (Touval, 1996). US Secretary of State James Baker's only trip to Yugoslavia occurred one week before Croatia and Slovenia declared independence. Despite the initially ambivalent attitude on the part of the USA and Baker's subsequent categorical statements in June 1991 warning against independence, the Croats and the Slovenes both declared independence.

The UN did later deploy troops to Croatia in 1992 after the violence erupted and after more than a third of Croatian territory was controlled by Serb forces. But the dominant view in Croatia and Bosnia at the time was that the UN Protection Force was doing little more than sanctioning Serb consolidation of Krajina and eastern Slavonia (Shoup, 1992; Gow, 1997, pp. 102–108).

Given all these factors, it is not clear that any 'norm of humanitarian intervention' existed in any significant and meaningful fashion in 1991 and 1992. In fact the explicit US statements and diplomatic démarches, coupled with the decisions by the USA not to intervene on behalf of either the Iraqi Shiite or Kurdish populations to aid their political ambitions, and to withdraw from Somalia, suggest that the more salient 'lesson' of the early 1990s was that there would be no international intervention without more tangible strategic interests at stake for the intervening state.

In the end, the actions by the Bosnians in 1992 were similar to those taken by Croatia and Slovenia a year earlier. Neither Slovenia nor Croatia expected international humanitarian intervention on its behalf before its declaration. Yet in both Slovenia and Croatia, once war broke out, Slovenian and Croatian leaders appealed for international support on their behalf. Similarly, once the war broke out in Bosnia, the Bosnian Muslims engaged in extensive efforts to solicit international intervention. But, in the run-up to the war, there is little evidence—either from their actions or from their words—to support the claim that this was the principal motivating factor behind their decisions to seek independence.

Kosovo.   The case of Kosovo is also problematic. Kuperman argues that "the rebels calculated that, if they could provoke Serb retaliation against Albanian civilians, the West would be compelled by media coverage of humanitarian tragedy (the 'CNN effect') to intervene despite its declarations" (Kuperman, 2006, p. 15). He adds that, although the USA and Europe repeatedly tried to deter the Albanians, these threats to withhold intervention "were not credible" (Kuperman, 2006, p. 15). But, as Grigorian (2006) discusses in his contribution to this volume, there is something puzzling about the fact that Western threats to withhold intervention were not credible· to the Kosovo Albanians because of the dominance of the norms of intervention, while these same norms were not sufficient to deter Serb military action against Kosovo. By definition, a norm is a shared understanding and expectation of appropriate action; why was the norm of intervention so effective in its incentive effect *vis-à-vis* the Kosovo Albanians and so weak in its deterrent effect *vis-à-vis* the Serbs?

Ironically, the more powerful case for moral hazard was a case in which the strongest conditions for moral hazard existed, but the dog did not bark. The 1992 Christmas warning to Belgrade by the Bush administration explicitly warned that the USA would be prepared to use military force if Milosevic took military action in Kosovo. Indeed, to the dismay of the leadership in Bosnia and Croatia, the US démarche clearly distinguished conflict in Kosovo as a different situation from the ongoing war in Bosnia. The Bush administration concluded that a Serb crack-down in Kosovo could trigger violence and spill over to neighbouring Macedonia, Bulgaria, Greece and even Turkey. Unlike in Bosnia, where the USA was still unwilling to intervene despite more than 100 000 dead and the disclosure of concentration-style camps in August 1992, violence spilling out of Kosovo and engulfing key NATO allies would be of significant strategic concern to the USA. Crawford ignores the possibility that the Christmas warning created moral hazard, instead suggesting it was a classic case of extended deterrence (Crawford, 2003, p. 177). But this raises the question: why didn't the warning to Belgrade trigger moral hazard? Why did it not signal to the Kosovo Albanians a green light to step up pressure on Milosevic given that the independence movement within Kosovo had been escalating its demands for independence from Belgrade for more than two decades? The démarche was widely publicized in the press at the time. US officials clearly intended to send a strong and credible message by explicitly declaring that Kosovo would be a "qualitatively different kind of problem than Bosnia" (Binder, 1992; Goshko, 1992).

What we are left with from the Kosovo case is the fact that, when an explicit threat was made to Belgrade that any use of military force in Kosovo would trigger international intervention, there was no provocation by the Kosovo Albanians. Conversely, six years later the international community and the USA explicitly warned the KLA that it would not intervene on their behalf, and yet we supposedly get the moral hazard.

This suggests that, at the very least, the model needs much more conceptual development, clearer specification of the variables, and more robust empirical testing. Norms and precedents are structural variables that should not vary from audience to audience. If norms are to be considered a motivating force for Bosnian Muslims in 1992, why were they not for Kosovo Albanians that same year—especially in light of the explicit diplomatic and public language of support for the latter? If there are variations in how audiences perceive international words and actions or variation in how various audiences establish their expectations of international intervention (e.g. Bosnian Muslims and the KLA allegedly expected intervention yet the Serbs remained undeterred), then the causal element can not be merely international action and norms.

The Positive Role of Norms

At best, we have a single case—Kosovo—which exhibits some evidence of the rebel group engaging in provocative action in hopes of luring international intervention on its behalf. But, as I have argued, there are some troubling conceptual and empirical issues even in this case. Bosnia does not appear to be a strong case to exhibit the conditions related to moral hazard, and the list of rebellions from 1945 to 1987 presented in Harff and Gurr cannot be classified as instances of victim groups provoking violence against themselves for the purposes of enlisting international intervention.

The argument and logic of moral hazard, however, must also contend with another consideration. Recent empirical evidence suggests that the number of internal wars, wars of secession and ethnic wars has declined over the past decade; at the same time the emerging norms of humanitarian intervention, human rights and democracy appear to have become more established (Eriksson & Wallensteen, 2004; Gurr, 2000). The rise in these types of war began in the 1980s and peaked in 1994—roughly corresponding with the decline of the Soviet empire, the rise of new nationalist and ethnic claims, and the reduction of Soviet and US subsidization of proxy regimes around the globe. Writing in 2000 Gurr found that, of the 59 ethnic conflicts in 1999, 23 were de-escalating while only seven were escalating (Gurr, 2000). Furthermore, Gurr found that the number of new wars each year has dropped significantly from that of the 1980s and early 1990s.

Several factors may be contributing to this decline. For example, there is some evidence that new international regimes and norms of sovereignty and minority rights are becoming more entrenched in intrastate negotiations and international diplomatic processes. Gurr argues that the emerging norms of humanitarian intervention over the past decade have coincided with a significant rise in the number of electoral democracies, new strategies of conflict resolution and newly established practices of governance (Gurr, 2000). While much more work needs to be done on these issues to establish a better sense of the broader trends and the causal factors behind them, the existing data suggest that, contrary to the theory of moral hazard, which highlights alleged pathologies of international intervention, norms of humanitarian intervention are making the world more stable. This is further evidence that the theory of moral hazard faces an uphill climb to become a useful tool in international relations theory.

References

Amnesty International (1985) *Yugoslav Prisoners of Conscience* (London: Amnesty International).

Betts, R. K. (1992) Systems for peace or causes of war? Collective security, arms control, and the new Europe, *International Security*, 17(1), pp. 5–43.

Binder, D. (1992) Bush warns Serbs not to widen war, *New York Times*, 28 December, p. A6.

Burg, S. L. & Shoup, P. S. (2000) *The War in Bosnia–Herzegovina: Ethnic Conflict and International Intervention* (New York: M.E. Sharpe).

Crawford, T. (2003) *Pivotal Deterrence: Third-Party Statecraft and the Pursuit of Peace* (Ithaca, NY: Cornell University Press).

Crawford, T. (2006) Moral hazard, intervention, and internal war: a conceptual analysis, in: T.W. Crawford and A.J. Kuperman (Eds.), *Gambling on Humanitarian Intervention* (London: Routledge).

Eriksson, M. & Wallensteen, P. (2004) Armed conflict, 1989–2003, *Journal of Peace Research*, 41(5), pp. 625–636.

Finnemore, M. (1996) Constructing norms of humanitarian intervention, in: P. Katzenstein (Ed.), *The Culture of National Security: Norms and Identity in World Politics*, pp. 153–185 (New York: Columbia University Press).

Finnemore, M. (2003) *The Purpose of Intervention: Changing Beliefs About the Use of Force* (Ithaca, NY: Cornell University Press).

Gagnon, V. P. (2004) *The Myth of Ethnic War: Serbia and Croatia in the 1990s* (Ithaca, NY: Cornell University Press).

Goshko, J. M. (1992) Bush threatens 'military force' if Serbs attack ethnic Albanians, *Washington Post*, 29 December, p. A10.

Gow, J. (1997) *Triumph of the Lack of Will: International Diplomacy and the Yugoslav War* (New York: Columbia University Press).

Grigorian, A. (2006) Third-party intervention and escalation in Kosovo: does moral hazard explain it?, in: T.W. Crawford and A.J. Kuperman (Eds.), *Gambling on Humanitarian Intervention* (London: Routledge).

Gurr, T. R. (2000) Ethnic warfare on the wane, *Foreign Affairs*, 79(3), pp. 52–64.

Harff, B. & Gurr, T. R. (1988) Toward empirical theory of genocides and politicides, *International Studies Quarterly*, 32, p. 359–371.

Khan, A. (2003) Baloch ethnic nationalism in Pakistan: from guerrilla war to nowhere?, *Asian Ethnicity*, 4(2), pp. 281–293.

Kier, E. & Mercer, J. (1996) Setting precedents in anarchy: military intervention and weapons of mass destruction, *International Security*, 20(4), pp. 77–106.

Kupchan, C. A. & Kupchan, C. (1991) Concerts, collective security and the future of Europe, *International Security*, 16(1), pp. 114–161.

Kuperman, A. J. (2006) Suicidal rebellions and the moral hazard of humanitarian intervention, in: T.W. Crawford and A.J. Kuperman (Eds.), *Gambling on Humanitarian Intervention* (London: Routledge).

Lavine, H. & Wechsler, J. (1940) *War Propaganda and the United States* (New Haven, CT: Yale University Press).

Mearsheimer, J. (1994) The false promise of international institutions, *International Security*, 19(3), pp. 5–49.

Mertus, J. (1998) *Kosovo: How Myths and Truths Started a War* (Berkeley, CA: University of California Press).

Moore, P. (1992) The International Relations of the Yugoslav Area, *RFE/RL Research Report*, 1(18), pp. 33–38.

Shoup, P. (1992) The UN force: a new actor in the Croatian–Serbian crisis, *RFE/RL Research Report*, 1(13), pp. 9–13.

Silber, L. & Little, A. (1997) *Yugoslavia: Death of a Nation* (New York: Penguin Books).

Touval, S. (1996) Lessons of preventive diplomacy in Yugoslavia, in: C. A. Crocker, F. O. Hampson & P. Aall (Eds), *Managing Global Chaos: Sources of and Responses to International Conflict*, pp. 403–418 (Washington, DC: United States Institute of Peace Press).

Tyler, P. E. (1991) US presses Iraq to accept UN force to protect Kurds, *New York Times*, 11 May, p. 4.

Wickham-Crowley, T. P. (1992) *Guerrillas and Revolution in Latin America: A Comparative Study of Insurgents and Regimes since 1956* (Princeton, NJ: Princeton University Press).

Woodward, S. (1995) *Balkan Tragedy: Chaos and Dissolution After the Cold War* (Washington, DC: Brookings Institution).

Zimmermann, W. (1999) *Origins of a Catastrophe* (New York: Times Books).

The Hazards of Thinking about Moral Hazard

R. HARRISON WAGNER

In a report published in 2001, written in response to controversies about military intervention in Somalia, Rwanda and the Balkans after the end of the Cold War, an international commission of some distinguished and influential people defended the idea of a global "responsibility to protect" states' populations from harm. "Where a population is suffering serious harm, as a result of internal war, insurgency, repression or state failure", the commission said, "and the state in question is unwilling or unable to halt or avert it", the principle of non-intervention must yield to the global responsibility to protect the people who would otherwise suffer, and intervention by other states may be required (International Commission on Intervention and State Sovereignty, 2001, p. xi). Alan Kuperman claims that the reasoning behind such demands for humanitarian intervention is incomplete, since it overlooks the possibility that expectations of intervention might increase the frequency of the problems intervention is intended to mitigate. "Intended as a type of insurance policy against genocidal violence", he claims, a norm of humanitarian intervention "exhibits the pathology of all insurance systems by creating moral hazard that encourages risk-taking" (Kuperman, 2006, p. 2). But what does humanitarian intervention have to do with insurance? Believe it or not, the game of baseball can help clarify our thoughts about this question.

Moral Hazard on the Mound?

Among the most interesting ideas of 2004, according to a recent issue of the *New York Times Magazine*, was an analysis of the rule in professional baseball allowing a "designated hitter" to replace a team's pitcher when it is the pitcher's turn to bat. "Baseball purists have long argued that the designated hitter is a moral outrage", said the article. "Now an economist and a mathematician have found that the D. H. is also a moral hazard" (Pink, 2004). Moral hazard, it appears, exists even on the baseball mound.

"In economics", according to the article in the *New York Times Magazine*, "'moral hazard' is the term for the idea that someone insured against risk is more likely to engage in risky behavior". A pitcher who does not have to bat need not fear retaliation from the opposing team's pitcher if he hits a batter. And therefore, the article says, "just as a homeowner who has fire insurance is more likely to risk smoking in bed . . . so, too, a pitcher who has a designated hitter batting in his stead is more likely to risk plunking an opposing player".

There are three questions one might ask about this claim. One is whether the term 'moral hazard' has been stretched too far if it is applied to an analysis of the effect of the designated hitter rule. A second is whether a good argument can actually be given to support the claim made about the effect of this rule. And a third is whether the rule actually has such an effect. An answer to the first question does not provide an answer to the second, nor does an answer to the second tell one the answer to the third.

The first question is not very interesting, except, perhaps, as part of a discussion of recent intellectual history. The *American Heritage Dictionary* defines moral hazard as "A risk to an insurance company resulting from uncertainty about the honesty of the insured". As the definition quoted above illustrates, the term has been extended to cover situations in which the insurance company risks, not fraud, but the possibility that people who are insured will simply take the insurance into account in deciding whether to take risks. And the article about the designated hitter illustrates the fact that now the term is sometimes applied to situations in which there is no insurance at all, but people just respond in unexpected and undesirable ways to actions that reduce the risks that they face.

However, not every instance of this last possibility is called 'moral hazard'. A well known article by Sam Peltzman, for example, argued that automobile safety regulations actually increased the number of automobile accidents, because they reduced the risk of personal injury that accidents entailed. While one could use the term 'moral hazard' to describe this effect, and Peltzman's article is cited in the paper on the designated hitter summarized in the *New York Times Magazine*, Peltzman did not use the term in his article (Peltzman, 1975).

As a general rule it seems plausible that if one reduces the risks associated with some behaviour, the frequency of the behaviour will increase. But whether one calls that effect 'moral hazard' or not, it is often difficult to show that such an effect occurs in any particular situation of interest. A person who tracked down the paper about the designated hitter discussed in the *New York Times Magazine*, for example, might be surprised to discover that there is a literature on this subject, and some controversy about whether the designated hitter rule actually has the effect attributed to it.

The fact that designated hitters are allowed in the American League but not the National League would appear to constitute a natural experiment allowing a test of this hypothesis, and in fact there are more batters hit by pitchers in the former than in the latter. Moreover, there are quotations from players that indicate they believe this effect exists (Bradbury & Drinen, 2003, p. 1). Nonetheless, some writers have been sceptical of the claim. They have pointed out that retaliating against a pitcher is costly, since hitting the pitcher with the ball has the effect of putting one of the poorest hitters on the opposing team on base. So pitchers may not actually have much to fear from retaliation. Moreover, since the whole point of the designated hitter rule is to allow a team to replace a poor-hitting pitcher with a good hitter, the greater number of batters hit by pitchers in the American League could be explained by the fact that the average net benefit of hitting batters is greater there.

Thus, even if we believe that reducing the risks associated with some behaviour will increase its frequency, we cannot conclude that the designated hitter rule will cause pitchers to feel freer to hit opposing batters, since the costs and benefits of hitting batters and retaliating if a batter is hit are both complex. That is the motivation for the research on the designated hitter rule discussed in the *New York Times Magazine* article.

There is an important lesson to be drawn from the designated hitter controversy: intuitive reasoning that is consistent with the known facts is not always enough to tell us how things work, since, if we think a little harder, we may find competing intuitions that are equally consistent with the facts. To find out which intuition is correct, we must look for facts that would be consistent with one guess but not another. But to do that we must often construct an explicit argument to show exactly what each would lead us to expect.

That is what the authors of the paper discussed in the *New York Times Magazine* set out to do: they tried to make explicit the cost–benefit calculations that the manager of a team would make in deciding how to respond to the designated hitter rule, and then found some new data that would help them discriminate between competing guesses as to what a manager would decide. They concluded that at least some of the difference between the American and the National Leagues in the number of batters hit by pitchers was the result of the lower fear of retaliation by pitchers in the American League (Bradbury & Drinen, 2003).

Humanitarian Intervention

The debate about the designated hitter rule provides a useful context for thinking about Kuperman's claim about moral hazard and humanitarian intervention. This claim appears to be consistent with both the intuitive reasoning associated with the notion of moral hazard described above, and much of the literature about it in economics. Moreover, like the claims made about the designated hitter rule, it is supported by what participants in recent conflicts in the Balkans and elsewhere have said about why they did what they did. Thus it deserves to be taken seriously.

Use of the term 'moral hazard' in the context of military intervention is itself hazardous, however, since it can lead one to believe that there is something like a theory of moral hazard that has been developed in economics that supports Kuperman's reasoning about the effect of humanitarian intervention. But that is no more true of humanitarian intervention than it was of the designated hitter rule in baseball, or of Peltzman's claims about the effects of automobile safety regulations. In order to determine whether humanitarian intervention leads to moral hazard, one must provide an analysis of the decisions made by parties to the conflicts that might prompt such intervention, and then determine what effect expectations about possible intervention by outsiders might have on them.

Robert Rauchhaus provides a summary of standard models of moral hazard in insurance constructed by economists, and concludes they are not much help in understanding the possible effects of intervention in violent conflicts (Rauchhaus, 2006). Arman Grigorian argues that the literature on the moral hazard associated with intervention has failed to capture the strategic complexity of conflicts like the one over Kosovo (Grigorian, 2006). However, neither Grigorian nor Rauchhaus provides an analysis that would tell us, like the paper on the designated hitter rule discussed above, how to think about the decisions made by the parties to domestic conflicts that might be influenced by expectations of outside intervention. Timothy Crawford focuses on when it is appropriate to speak of moral hazard, not on whether there is an argument to support the claim made by Kuperman and others that the possibility of outside intervention produces it (Crawford, 2006).

Kuperman's discussion of how to take moral hazard into account in deciding when to intervene is based on the literature in economics on insurance and regulation (Kuperman, 2006, pp. 12–18), but his argument for the existence of moral hazard, he says, is based on "rational deterrence theory from international relations" (2006, p. 8). His claim is that the expectation of outside intervention weakens the ability of governments to deter rebellions "by threatening massive retaliation" (Kuperman, 2006, p. 9). But this claim is rather odd in the context of a situation in which potential intervenors are trying to deter *governments* from engaging in genocide, since it is not clear why governments could not be deterred from responding to rebellions with genocide, or why rebellions would occur if governments were deterred from doing harm to their subjects.[1] And it is not clear whether reasoning that might be supported by some analysis of attempts by governments to deter rebellions would be consistent with policy recommendations that might be derived from the economics literature on optimal insurance contracts.

I think one is forced to conclude that the literature on moral hazard and humanitarian intervention has not yet reached the level of sophistication of the literature on the designated hitter rule in baseball. One reason for this is that the issues raised by Kuperman and others who have written on this subject are not only important, but also extremely complex. Therefore it is far harder to provide an account of the relevant decisions in the context of humanitarian intervention than it is to analyse how a baseball manager might decide how to respond to the designated hitter rule. While I am in no position to provide such an analysis here, I will sketch out how I believe one might begin to think about it, both to illustrate the complexity of the issues and, perhaps, to provide a stimulus to a more complete analysis.[2]

Constitutional Bargains

Thomas Schelling once wrote:

> The tyrant and his subjects are in somewhat symmetrical positions. *They* can deny *him* most of what *he* wants ... and *he* can deny *them* just about everything *they* want—he can deny it by using the force at his command ... [while] they can deny him the economic fruits of conquest ... It is a bargaining situation in which either side, if adequately disciplined and organized, can deny most of what the

other wants; and it remains to see who wins. (Quoted in Ackerman & Kruegler, 1994, p. 9, emphasis in the original)

If we think of the relation between ruler and ruled in this way, then the organisation of the state can be thought of as a contract, in which the ruler provides public goods in exchange for taxes, and the terms of this contract are influenced by the relative bargaining power of ruler and ruled.

Thus changes in the relative bargaining power of ruler and ruled provide an opportunity to renegotiate the terms of their relationship. But violent bargaining, like any other bargaining, is inefficient for both sides. Therefore, as the book in which Schelling's statement is quoted was at pains to emphasize, this renegotiation need not involve violence. Like interstate bargaining, however, the bargaining between ruler and ruled takes place in the shadow of organized violence, even when violence does not occur, and is subject to the same sources of inefficiency. Thus violence cannot be ruled out.

The sources of inefficiency in interstate bargaining have been most clearly identified in James Fearon's well-known article on the subject (Fearon, 1995). Fearon divided these sources of inefficiency into three categories: indivisibility of the stakes; misrepresentation of private information about capabilities or values; and the inability of a party to a conflict to commit itself to abide by the terms of an agreement it might accept in lieu of violence.

If what is at stake in a conflict is indivisible, then there is no intermediate outcome between complete victory for one side and complete victory for the other, and therefore no alternative available that both sides might prefer to a contest leading to one of those outcomes. Many people have thought that this must usually be true of intrastate conflicts, since they are about who will rule. But the point of a constitution is to avoid this stark choice by determining how rulers are chosen and what they can and cannot do, and therefore it is not necessarily impossible to renegotiate a constitutional bargain to reflect a change in the distribution of bargaining power among the parties to domestic conflicts. To explain why this does not happen peacefully, the focus of attention should therefore usually be on the other two sources of inefficiency.[3]

I would argue that the second source of inefficiency listed by Fearon, the misrepresentation of private information about capabilities or values, is just one possible explanation for the existence of a more general problem: inconsistent expectations about the outcome of violent conflicts, or about how relevant actors will respond to them. Clearly the parties to such conflicts have an incentive to exaggerate both their military capabilities and the value they place on their demands, but, even if each could read the minds of the others, they might still disagree about how a conflict would unfold if it continued. It seems unlikely, for example, that the only possible source of disagreement about the efficacy of suicide bombing as a strategy for achieving a group's goals in the Middle East is misrepresentation by political leaders of how sensitive they really are to the deaths caused by such bombings.[4] But, whatever the source of such inconsistent expectations, observation of the effects of violence may be the only way that these can be revised until they are consistent enough for there to be a settlement that all the parties to the conflict would prefer to continuing it.[5]

Even if there is some agreement that all the parties to a conflict would prefer to violence, acceptance of it might lead to a worsened bargaining position for one or more of the parties to it in subsequent conflicts. If the advantaged party cannot commit itself to abide by the terms of the original agreement, then the party that expects to be disadvantaged in the future may not accept it. If a group's adversary is expected to become stronger, for example, and an agreement will not prevent that, then the group may prefer to use violence to try to weaken its adversary before it becomes stronger. Or an agreement may itself imply a worsening of the bargaining position of a group—if it has to disarm, for example, or cede strategic territory to another group—in which case the group that expects to be disadvantaged may refuse to accept an agreement it would otherwise have preferred to continued violence.

These commitment problems are also called enforcement problems, and they are familiar to students of international politics, among whom it is commonly accepted that agreements among independent states must be self-enforcing. But, contrary to what many students of international politics have written, these problems are actually more serious in intrastate conflicts, where acceptance of a constitutional bargain typically requires giving some organization a monopoly of the legitimate use of violence and finding some way to insure that it does not use that monopoly to renege on the agreement that created it. In fact, one way of making a hazardous agreement among the parties to a violent conflict self-enforcing is to allow them not to disarm, by partitioning a state into two or more separate states. This is ironic, since many students of international politics regard anarchy—i.e. the absence of a monopoly of the legitimate use of force at the global level—as a cause of war, not peace.[6]

In intrastate conflicts there may also be a fourth barrier to agreement—a lack of consolidation of one or more parties—although one could argue that it is not really a separate category, but just another source of inconsistent expectations or commitment problems. This fourth barrier does not exist in interstate conflicts because governments that enjoy a monopoly of the legitimate use of force within their territories can not only make war, they can also make peace. All that is needed to avoid or end interstate war is to find an agreement that the contending states all prefer to fighting. By contrast, in intrastate conflicts the formation of groups may be endogenous to the conflict and, while the participants may be able to coordinate their actions sufficiently to fight each other, there may be no one able to call off the fighting. The point of violence in these circumstances may not be to weaken the enemy or persuade it to make a concession, but to attract more support for one's organization or punish defectors from it. This is another reason why conflicts between or among governments may actually be easier to resolve than conflicts within states.

Moreover, some internal conflicts commonly called civil wars may not actually be contests to determine the terms of a contract between ruler and ruled at all, but may instead be just a general condition of lawlessness in which shifting groups compete with each other for control over valuable resources, and armies in government uniforms do the same thing. Territories in such a condition have a much stronger claim to be called 'anarchic' than does the system of great powers which students of international politics have often characterized by that term.

The report of the International Commission on Intervention and State Sovereignty illustrates the fact that outsiders have always been parties to the contract that defines a state. Indeed, part of the definition of a state is that its internal sovereignty is recognized by other states. Therefore the contract that defines a state reflects not only the relative bargaining power of groups within its territory, but also the relative bargaining power between them and outsiders, and the distribution of bargaining power among the outsiders. Calls for humanitarian military intervention are demands that outsiders participate in the renegotiation of the contracts that define a state. And attempts to specify basic human rights at the global level are efforts to define certain minimum conditions that all such contracts should satisfy.

Debates about humanitarian military intervention therefore implicitly raise two sets of questions. One concerns what sorts of constitutional contracts would be consistent with the actual distribution of bargaining power among the groups that might engage in forceful bargaining over their terms. The other concerns how much violence any attempt to renegotiate the terms of some particular constitutional contract would entail, and who would be required to participate in it. There are therefore two different ways in which 'idealistic' attempts to specify human rights at the global level might be 'unrealistic' or 'utopian': they might imply unrealistic expectations about what is actually feasible, and they might underestimate the amount of violence that would be required to enforce such rights, even if they could be enforced.[7]

In practice, decisions to intervene are influenced by answers to both these questions. As a result, it is difficult to anticipate which states might decide to intervene in which local conflicts. This is why the possibility of humanitarian intervention could make intrastate violent conflicts more likely, as Kuperman claims. But this effect has little to do with moral hazard, even in the extended sense of that term exemplified by the debate about the designated hitter rule.

The Hazards of Doing Good

Since inconsistent expectations about how a violent conflict would unfold can make the peaceful renegotiation of constitutional bargains impossible, inconsistent expectations about how potential outside intervenors might respond to such conflicts can make it impossible for conflicting groups within a state's territory to settle their conflicts peacefully. Less obviously, since outside intervention, if it occurs, would lead to a drastic change in the relative bargaining power of ruler and ruled, rulers may have an incentive to take preventive or pre-emptive action against dissident groups if they have reason to believe that doing so would remove the incentive of outsiders to intervene. Rulers might, for example, believe that, if sufficient numbers of the dissidents were killed, or their organization sufficiently weakened, there would no longer be an incentive for outsiders to intervene to protect them, or that any intervention that occurred would have little effect on the long-term ability of the ruling group to maintain its dominant position.

Neither inconsistent beliefs about the likelihood of intervention (or its effects), nor the incentive to pre-empt it, however, could plausibly be said to be simply the result of outsiders' insuring domestic dissidents against immediate harm (where such insurance might or might not turn out to be reliable). Each would instead be the result of encouraging dissidents to believe that any immediate harm that they suffered would lead to significant long-run benefits, in the form of a change in the terms of the constitutional bargain between rulers and ruled. And that would be true even if the sole objective of the intervenors were to protect the dissidents from harm, since limiting the harm that rulers can do to their subjects changes the relative bargaining power of ruler and ruled, and therefore enables the ruled to demand changes in the terms of their relationship.[8] In the first case the violence would be the consequence of the fact that the ruling group was not as confident that outsiders would intervene decisively as were the dissidents, and therefore preferred to fight rather than make the concessions demanded. In the second case the violence would be the result of the fact that the ruling group believed that intervention was sufficiently likely to warrant taking preventive or pre-emptive measures which would allow it to avoid the concessions that would be required if intervention occurred. The first effect could be reliably avoided only if the ability and willingness of outsiders to intervene to enforce well specified constitutional standards were commonly known by all possible participants in intrastate conflicts. I see no way such a condition could be satisfied, no matter how many commission reports are written or Security Council resolutions are adopted. And, even then, the result might be an unknown number of preventive or pre-emptive acts of repression by rulers who were persuaded that outside intervention would otherwise occur.

Note how different this is from the moral hazard that results from insurance. The more reliable an insurance policy is, the greater the problem of moral hazard. But the more credible and specific a norm of humanitarian intervention became, the less likely would be inconsistent expectations about whether it would occur and what its consequences would be. Of course, preventive or pre-emptive attacks might become more likely, but they do not resemble moral hazard at all.[9]

In light of the costliness of humanitarian intervention, and the consequent opposition it arouses among some constituents of the potential intervenors, the opposite possibility might be worth considering: a clear commitment not to intervene, which might be more credible. This is, of course, just another way of phrasing the norm of non-intervention. The price of such a commitment, of course, would be acceptance of whatever horrors might be perpetrated by governments, as long as they did not threaten the interests of citizens of other states. But such a commitment might nonetheless avoid both the domestic violence that could result from unrealistic expectations of outside support on the part of domestic dissidents, and acts of preventive or pre-emptive violence by rulers who sought to forestall it. There is a difficult trade-off to be made here, but we cannot rule out the possibility that non-intervention would be the more desirable rule. This possibility would be consistent with what is by now a familiar theme in the economics literature on economic policy. It is obvious that it is desirable to find ways to tie governments' hands so that they cannot do harm. It is not so obvious, but nonetheless sometimes true, that it can be useful to tie governments' hands so that they cannot do good.

Sometimes this is true because doing good leads to something that could plausibly be called moral hazard, but not always. Finn Kydland and Edward Prescott, for example, recently received the Nobel Prize in economics, in part for work that demonstrated that, if a government always responds optimally to the current level of inflation or unemployment, the result will be suboptimal levels of inflation or unemployment over time. The reason is not moral hazard, but just the fact that such actions fail to take into account how economic agents would respond to the expectation that the government would act in that way. If one takes the reaction of economic actors to government policy into account, they argued, it can be socially beneficial to restrict the discretion that even well-meaning governments have in making economic policy (Kydland & Prescott, 1977). The norm of non-intervention, if it is effective, might possibly be justified in the same way. Of course, because of what has been called the 'CNN effect', it may be no more possible for outsiders to commit themselves credibly not to intervene than it is to commit themselves to intervene. The norm of non-intervention reflected the distribution of bargaining power among the major powers, and between them and dissident groups within states. It is in part because the spread of nationalism made intervention by outsiders very costly, and interventions in the past led to conflicts among the major powers over who would intervene where, that non-intervention had as much support as it did.[10]

The end of the Cold War seemed to end the prospect of military conflict among the major states, and left the members of NATO with a very large military force that had no clear immediate use. Thus some people began to think that humanitarian intervention might be both easy and non-controversial. Such optimism is harder to sustain in light of both the recent war in Iraq and the lingering problems from earlier interventions in the Balkans. Thus the norm of non-intervention might be given new life for reasons that have little to do with the possibility that its abandonment could be a stimulus to intrastate violence.

States will, of course, continue to intervene when they think their interests require it. But that does not make international norms irrelevant, since norms provide a focal point for coordinating the reactions of other states and of democratic publics. They will therefore influence the costs and benefits that are weighed in deciding whether to intervene in any particular conflict. Thus it is still relevant to ask whether it is better to make it easy to justify intervention (as a global 'responsibility to protect' would do), or hard to justify it (as the principle of non-intervention has done). Moreover, as the deterrence literature emphasizes, individual acts of intervention influence expectations of what states will do in subsequent conflicts, and states need to take this into account in deciding whether to intervene in any particular conflict.

These, I think, are the issues that are raised by Alan Kuperman's work on humanitarian intervention. It seems clear that they are not only practically important, but theoretically significant as well.

Acknowledgements

I would like to thank Alan Kessler, Pat McDonald and Robert Rauchhaus for their comments on earlier versions of this paper, and Alan Kuperman and Tim Crawford for helpful editorial suggestions.

Notes

1. These questions are also raised in Grigorian (2006) and Rauchhaus (2006).
2. A preliminary version of some of these ideas can be found in Wagner (2004). A more extended version is presented in Wagner (2005).
3. It is important to bear in mind, however, that the fact that possible compromise settlements are available does not alone guarantee that there will be some compromise that everyone would prefer to a winner-take-all contest (Fearon, 1995, pp. 386–388). If no feasible agreement is jointly preferred to a contest, then a contest would not be inefficient.
4. Fearon acknowledges that such inconsistent expectations may exist, but attributes them to "bounded rationality", which seems to imply that fully rational decision makers with the same information would always have consistent expectations (Fearon, 1995, pp. 392–393). But since personal or subjective probabilities just reflect people's preferences between lotteries with known probabilities and uncertain outcomes with unknown probabilities, it is not clear in what way such incompatible expectations are inconsistent with rational behaviour, or how they could be avoided by rational decision makers.
5. This is the central theme of much of the recent literature on the relation between war and bargaining. The idea can be found in Clausewitz (1976), and is the main theme of Blainey (1988). Note, however, that, while Blainey popularized the idea that states may have conflicting beliefs about their relative military capabilities, conflicting beliefs about the distribution of the costs of war may be at least as important. For a fuller discussion and further references, see Wagner (2000). See also Muthoo (2000).

6. For an extended discussion, see Wagner (2005).
7. For a more extended discussion of the familiar contrast between 'idealism' and 'realism' in writings about politics, see *ibid*.
8. This is perhaps what Kuperman has in mind when he says that a norm of humanitarian intervention would undermine the ability of rulers to deter rebellion by threatening massive retaliation.
9. My thanks to Pat McDonald for helping me see this point more clearly. For a discussion of how other forms of humanitarian involvement in intrastate military conflicts can also have unexpected adverse consequences, see Terry (2002).
10. See the discussion by Marc Trachtenberg (1993) of exceptions to the norm of non-intervention in the 19th and early 20th centuries.

References

Ackerman, P. & Kruegler, C. (1994) *Strategic Nonviolent Conflict: The Dynamics of People Power in the Twentieth Century* (Westport, CT: Praeger Publishers).

Blainey, G. (1988) *The Causes of War* (New York: Free Press).

Bradbury, J. C. & Drinen, D. (2003) Moral hazard on the mound: the economics of plunking, unpublished paper, Department of Economics, University of the South, Sewanee, TN, August.

von Clausewitz, C. (1976) *On War* (originally published in 1832), ed. and trans. Michael Howard and Peter Paret (Princeton, NJ: Princeton University Press).

Crawford, T. W. (2006) Moral hazard, intervention and internal war: a conceptual analysis, in: T.W. Crawford and A.J. Kuperman (Eds.), *Gambling on Humanitarian Intervention* (London: Routledge).

Fearon, J. D. (1995) Rationalist explanations for war, *International Organization*, 49(3), pp. 379–414.

Grigorian, A. (2006) Third-party intervention and escalation in Kosovo: does moral hazard explain it?, in: T.W. Crawford and A.J. Kuperman (Eds.), *Gambling on Humanitarian Intervention* (London: Routledge).

International Commission on Intervention and State Sovereignty (2001) *The Responsibility to Protect*, International Development Research Center, Ottawa, available online at: http://www.dfait-maeci.gc.ca/iciss-ciise/menu-en.asp.

Kuperman, A. J. (2006) Suicidal rebellions and the moral hazard of humanitarian intervention, in: T.W. Crawford and A.J. Kuperman (Eds.), *Gambling on Humanitarian Intervention* (London: Routledge).

Kydland, F. E. & Prescott, E. C. (1977) Rules rather than discretion: the inconsistency of optimal plans, *Journal of Political Economy*, 85(3), pp. 473–492.

Muthoo, A. (2000) A non-technical introduction to bargaining theory, *World Economics*, 1(2), pp. 145–166.

Peltzman, S. (1975) The effects of automobile safety regulation, *Journal of Political Economy*, 83(4), pp. 677–726.

Pink, D. H. (2004) The designated hitter as moral hazard, *New York Times Magazine*, 12 December, available online at: http://www.nytimes.com/2004/12/12/magazine/12DESIGNATED.html?oref=login&page.

Rauchhaus, R. W. (2006) Humanitarian intervention, conflict management and the application and misapplication of moral hazard theory, in: T.W. Crawford and A.J. Kuperman (Eds.), *Gambling on Humanitarian Intervention* (London: Routledge).

Terry, F. (2002) *Condemned to Repeat? The Paradox of Humanitarian Action* (Ithaca, NY: Cornell University Press).

Trachtenberg, M. (1993) Intervention in historical perspective, in: L. W. Reed & C. Kaysen (Eds), *Emerging Norms of Justified Intervention* (Cambridge, MA: American Academy of Arts and Sciences).

Wagner, R. H. (2000) Bargaining and war, *American Journal of Political Science*, 44(3), pp. 469–484.

Wagner, R. H. (2004) Bargaining and conflict management, in: Z. Maoz *et al.* (Eds), *Multiple Paths to Knowledge in International Relations* (New York: Lexington Books).

Wagner, R. H. (2005) War and the state: rethinking the theory of international politics, unpublished book-length manuscript, Department of Government, the University of Texas at Austin.

Index